Fenway!

Fenway!

The Ultimate Fan's Guide to the Nation's Ballpark

Tim Shea

Tasora Books
Minneapolis, Minnesota

Cover photo copyright ©2007 by Steady Photography, steadyphotography.com

All other photos copyright © 2007 by Tim Shea

To contact the publisher or author, email fenwayguide@yahoo.com.

The text is set in Goudy Old Style and Franklin Gothic Book.

This book is not endorsed by the Boston Red Sox or Fenway Park.

Published by Tasora Books
3501 Highway 100 South, Suite 220
Minneapolis, MN 55416
Phone: 1-800-901-3480

Printed in the United States of America
First printing, April 2007

ISBN 13:978-0-9789946-4-8
ISBN 10: 0-9789946-4-7

Library of Congress Control Number: 2007923187

10 9 8 7 6 5 4 3 2 1

Contents

Introduction

Be they friend or foe of The Nation, any fan who experiences a Sox game at Fenway immediately knows they are enjoying the greatest park ever to grace the baseball landscape. The wonderfully inexplicable outfield dimensions, the fabled Green Monster, and the positively palpable scent of history tells the visitor that this certainly is the most glorious baseball home every built, added on to, renovated, and reinvigorated.

Opened in 1912, Fenway has been a second home to New England baseball fans for almost a century. In the late 1990s, the caretaker owners devised a plan to build a new $665 million "Fenway Park" adjacent to the real Fenway. They said renovation would be too costly and impractical, and they wanted to improve the ballgame experience for all fans by giving them access to better amenities and more comfortable seats.

Thankfully, the ownership group that purchased the team and Fenway Park for $700 million in 2002 had the foresight and decency to discard any notions of building a new Fenway Park.

Incrementally over the past five years the new owners, guided by the architectural wizardry of Vice President of Planning and Development Janet Marie Smith, have done a superb job renovating and enhancing the fan experience through a variety of improvements. The famous Green Monster seats and Right Field Roof Deck Restaurant are two of the most dramatic additions, but there have been countless other subtle and creative changes, including greatly improving the variety and quality of food available, and clearing out storage areas to increase the public areas away from the seating.

In July 2005 the Red Sox applied to the National Park Service to have Fenway placed on the National Register of Historic Places. The process for being added to the register can take several years.

A great benefit to the team of having Fenway Park placed on the National Register of Historic Places would be the accompanying rehabilitation tax credits from the federal government. The team is in the midst of a 10-year, $200 million renovation of the park, and if the tax credits are realized it could save the team tens of millions of dollars, according to an August 2005 article in *The Boston Globe*.

Red Sox team president Larry Lucchino has said on many occasions that the ownership's mission is to improve Fenway Park while staunchly protecting its history and character.

"It's a modernization of Fenway while still being faithful to its charms and history. I think, at the end of the day, it's going to be one of our signature accomplishments that we've been able to modernize and improve Fenway and still preserve and protect the essence at Fenway. We're pretty proud of what we've done so far. We're on the right track. It's going to get bigger and better as we create more room," Lucchino said in October 2005.

"It is an honor to have the opportunity to protect and preserve Fenway Park," said John Henry, the team's principal owner, in March 2005. "We see how its history and charm attract people from all over the world, and how it helps connect generations within families."

What separates the current Red Sox owners from their predecessors is that they realize Fenway Park is both an irreplaceable treasure and the primary asset of their business. By investing $200 million into park improvements they are simultaneously increasing revenue through new seating and concessions. Consequently, the team has more money it can spend on player salaries, and if they make the right decisions on players, the team plays better, fans want to come to the games more than ever, and the sellout streak continues.

For the 2007 season, the team has opened up a notoriously cramped walkway behind the grandstand sections in left field. There will be a spacious new concession area, a standing room deck, and a ladies restroom in this area that used to be nothing more than a stiflingly crowded 4-foot wide aisle. The team is also building a Bleacher Bar and Restaurant under the center field bleachers and hopes to have it open by the middle of the 2007 season. The bar and restaurant will have a view of the field through what used to be the large opening for the park's audio speakers. The plan is to keep it open year-round so fans can go there to eat and drink and view the field.

About half of the luxury boxes were also renovated prior to the start of the 2007 season and the team plans to renovate the rest before the start of the 2008 season.

More than ever, Fenway is now a baseball paradise. It is a destination unto itself, and the fact that the home team is consistently good only adds to the enjoyment. The food and beverage options have been multiplied and enhanced to suit every taste. The improvements also extend beyond the walls of Fenway itself, as even the famous Cask'n'Flagon, once mainly a spot to grab a cold one before, after, or instead of, a game, now smacks of gentility with its dining tables on a veranda that look out upon the back of the Monster.

While the improvements to the park over the past several years have astounded all observers, there is one ancient element that still causes fans consternation: the infamous poles. Needed to support the park's second level, which now includes the press box, luxury boxes, pavilion seating, and the tony new EMC Club, the poles at Fenway are legendary for their ability to make you move backward, forward, and sideways in your seat so you don't miss key moments of the action.

There are many different types of seats at Fenway: Field Box, Loge Box, Outfield Box, Grandstand, Bleachers, Green Monster seats, Right Field Roof Box seats, and more. However, it is only the Grandstand Seats that have poles between the fans and the action on the field. Since most of the box seats are owned by season ticket holders, the average fan most often finds himself buying Grandstand or Bleacher seats. Some of the seats that are located behind poles are marked Obstructed View; others may not be.

In addition to providing useful information about how to get the most out of your Fenway experience, this book will help you identify those seats that have a pole impeding the view of home plate or the pitcher's mound, which is where the average fan's attention is focused during the majority of a game. Some fans may be surprised to learn that only about 3 percent of all the Grandstand seats have significant pole issues. That statistic, however, is not likely to be very comforting to the fans sitting behind a pole.

Some Facts about the Poles

- There are 26 steel poles positioned between the Loge Box and Right Field Box seats (red) and Grandstand seats (blue).
- Each pole is painted green and is about 16 inches wide.
- They are evenly spaced around Fenway, from sections 1 to 33.

How to Get Tickets

Having a great time at Fenway is a very easy thing to do. Getting tickets to the game you want to see, however, can be very difficult, frustrating, or expensive. The Sox are the toughest ticket in baseball, having sold out every home game since early in the 2003 season and the team currently holds the second longest consecutive-games sellout streak in baseball history. If the streak continues they will break the Cleveland Indians all-time mark of 444 consecutive sellouts in August 2008.

Numerous factors contribute to the scarcity of available tickets: the allure of Fenway Park itself; the incredible improvements made to the park in recent years; its capacity being one of the smallest in baseball; the increased fervor generated by the 2004 World Series championship; and the high number of season ticket holders (there is currently a waiting list to buy season tickets). Combine all of that with the legendary zeal New Englanders have for their favorite team and you begin to understand why it is such a hot ticket.

Having one of the smallest seating capacities in baseball, as well as the second highest player payroll, an unparalleled demand for tickets, and the team paying for $100 million of improvements to the park over the past five years have led to the Red Sox having the highest average ticket price in the game. The face value of the average ticket at Fenway for 2007 is about $47, which is about twice the average price amongst all major league ballparks. The average ticket for a Kansas City Royals home game is about $14, but as the cliché goes, you get what you pay for.

The price of tickets at Fenway actually varies from $12 for an upper bleacher seat to $312 for an infield dugout box seat.

However, the team has taken steps in the past few years to keep the cost of most tickets down so average families will not be priced out of the experience of attending a Sox game at Fenway. About 2/3 of all the seats in Fenway are either Infield Grandstand, Outfield Grandstand, and Bleachers. Prices for these tickets have not risen in at least three years, being $45, $27, and $23, respectively. The team has also not raised prices in several years for Right Field Box ($45), Right Field Roof Box Seats ($45), and general standing room ($20). In addition, the team continues to offer several hundred seats in the top rows of the bleachers for $12 each. While very hard to get, these tickets are certainly the best bargain in baseball.

The team's ticket pricing strategy over the past few years has been to continue to incrementally raise the prices of the most expensive seats (most of which are owned by season ticket holders), while freezing the prices of seats most often purchased for individual games.

There are many different ways to obtain tickets, whether you buy them directly from the team at face value or from a reseller at a premium price. Of course, buying tickets directly from the team rather than a reseller will almost always be the least expensive and safest way to get tickets.

Buying directly from the Red Sox

On sale dates, Sox Pax, and group tickets

If you want to increase your chances of getting tickets you should start paying attention in early December when the team usually puts the first batch of tickets on sale. Over the last several years

Typical Timeline for Red Sox Ticket Sales

Early December	Tickets for about 25 games in April, May, and September, as well as Sox Pax, go on sale
Mid-January	Group tickets (generally only available to prior group ticket buyers)
Late January	Tickets for rest of season, excluding Opening Day, Patriot's Day, and all Yankee games
February or early March	Lotteries for: Opening Day Patriots Day All Yankee games Green Monster seats (all games) Right Field Roof Deck (all games)
Day of game/week of game tickets	There are usually a few hundred held back for walkup sales, online, or telephone – start checking with ticket office and online a few days before the game
Ongoing during season	Red Sox Replay: season ticket holders sell tickets at face value through the team's Web site (very limited availability)

the team has put tickets for 20 to 25 games on sale about two weeks before Christmas, usually on the second Saturday in December. These are always games in April, May, and September, and most of them are on weeknights (and they include no Yankee games). In other words: school nights with the potential for chilly or rainy weather. This was first done a few years ago as a way to ensure sellouts of April weeknight games which are the hardest games for the team to sell out. Now that sellouts of every game are virtually assured for the foreseeable future, this December on sale date serves the purpose of staggering the on sale dates to give fans more opportunities, and giving fans a chance to buy tickets before the holidays so they can give them as gifts.

The tickets for this December on sale date are sold almost entirely through redsox.com and the 24-hour touchtone ticketing system (617-482-4769). For the past four years the team has been holding an event called "Christmas at Fenway" to coincide with the December ticket sale. During this event fans are allowed into Fenway Park to buy tickets and see some Red Sox players. Due to space restrictions caused by off-season construction, the December 2006 event was limited to fans who were awarded entry through an online lottery. As with any Red Sox on sale date, the vast majority of available tickets usually sell out in a day or less.

The Sox Pax are an excellent deal if you are able to get your hands on one. They consist of tickets to 4 games, with at least one or two being a highly sought after game such as the Yankees or Opening Day. There are up to 10 different game sets available, and the Sox Pax usually go on sale the same morning as "Christmas at Fenway." There are a limited number of Sox Pax available, so check redsox.com or call the ticket office (877-733-7699) in early December for more information.

Group ticket sales (20 or more for one game) are a great

opportunity if you are able to buy them. They usually go on sale in January before tickets for most games are made available to the general public. Group sales are very limited, and due to high demand, the team has had a policy the past several years of selling the majority of group sales to people or organizations that have purchased group tickets in the past. Call the ticket office (877-733-7699) in December or January for more information.

Tickets for the remainder of the regular season–with the exception of Opening Day and all Yankee games–typically go on sale on a Saturday morning in late January or early February. About 40 to 45 games are available, including all the prime weekend and summer games. Tickets for this on sale date are mainly sold at redsox.com or through the 24-hour touchtone ticketing system (617-482-4769). At the appointed time, legions of fans across New England punch up their Web browsers and sit in the "Virtual Waiting Room" for anywhere from 2 minutes to 20 hours. Many fans never make it to the spine-tingling moment when they actually see tickets offered to them on the Web site. By the end of the day or early the next morning, the Red Sox regular season is basically sold out, and fans who got nothing or didn't get the games they wanted have to look to other ways to obtain tickets.

Opening Day, Patriots' Day, Yankee games, Green Monster seats, and Right Field Roof Restaurant

Some tickets are so highly sought after that the team decided a few years ago to make the opportunity to purchase tickets to them available only through a lottery system. By doing this, they hope to increase the chances of average fans getting tickets to the best games and some of the best seats in the park. This includes all tickets to the 9 or 10 Yankee games each year, as well as Green Monster and Right Field Roof Restaurant tickets to all 81 home games. Tickets for Opening Day and Patriot's Day (a holiday in Massachusetts when they run the Boston Marathon and the Red Sox play a home game that starts in the morning) are also available only through lotteries. Through a series of staggered lottery drawings in February and early March, lucky fans who win the lottery are given the opportunity to come back to redsox.com at a specific time and purchase tickets with a special passcode. Fans who win one of the lotteries are usually allowed to buy four tickets to one game.

Buying tickets during the season

Once the season begins in April there is an excellent chance that each home game could already be classified as a sellout. However, there are still some opportunities for buying tickets from the team if you are patient and persistent. Some levels of membership to Red Sox Nation, the official team fan club (redsoxnation.com), include tickets to a game or the opportunity to buy tickets. For 2007, a $99.95 Red Sox Nation membership includes 2 tickets to a game (the tickets included are valued at $27 each, and most of the eligible games were in June, July, and August). **For $199, a Red Sox Nation Monster membership includes the guaranteed opportunity to purchase 2 Green Monster tickets to a game.** However, the Monster memberships quickly sold out. As with any Red Sox ticket buying opportunity, you are encouraged to act quickly if you are interested in obtaining tickets through a Red Sox Nation membership. Start checking the Red Sox Web site for information about memberships in November and December.

If you have the ability to be spontaneous and can decide to go a few days before or the day of a game, the Red Sox usually release a few hundred tickets a few days before or the day of a game. The team does hold back tickets until a day or two before the game for various reasons, including meeting the potential ticket needs of VIPs, of visiting teams, and handicapped accessible seating. Often they have held back more tickets than are required to meet those needs and some of the remaining tickets are released one to three days before each game. Check redsox.com or call the ticket office (877-733-7699) regularly for availability. You can also call the 24-hour touch tone ticketing system at 617-782-4769. There is no standard time or method by which the team releases tickets close to a game. Tickets are coded in the ticket office for Web sale, box office sale, phone sale, or day of game walkup sale. You are advised to check as many different types of sale as you can, and do so at different times of the day.

Day of Game Walkup Sales

It is a long-standing tradition that the Red Sox sell tickets on game day to individuals who walk up to the park. Here are the rules:

- Day of game tickets are only sold at the ticket window at Gate C on Lansdowne Street
- The team starts selling tickets 2 hours before game time, which is when the gates open for fans
- You are not supposed to line up for tickets until 5 hours before game time
- You cannot save a place in line for anyone
- You can only buy one ticket, for yourself, and you must go into the game immediately after buying your ticket

On an average game day, the team will sell anywhere from 50 to 300 tickets through this method. And yes, you can get into Yankee games by waiting in line on the day of the game. The team often hands out numbered wrist bands to the fans in line several hours before putting the tickets on sale.

If you want to get a day of game ticket you should go to Gate C about 6 hours before game time and look to see if there is a line forming. If there is no line, you can come back a little later. Just because you are in line does not mean you will definitely get a ticket, so you want to be as close to the front of the line as possible.

Red Sox Replay

This is an online system which allows fans to buy individual game tickets from Red Sox season ticket holders at face value, plus a service charge. Fans must pay $50 (once a year) to have the opportunity to buy the tickets when they are posted. It is unpredictable how many tickets will be made available through this site, but the availability is usually in direct correlation to the success of the team. When the Red Sox played poorly in August and September 2006 and were knocked out of playoff contention, there were many more tickets available through this method than at any other time during the year. For more information, check redsox.com or call 877-733-7699.

So, regarding getting tickets during the season, the message is: keep trying. Don't give up just because it appears the season is sold out and you think you may be stuck paying double face value (or more) for tickets from a reseller.

Season Tickets

The Red Sox have a season ticket waiting list. Fans can join the list for a fee of $50. As of March 2007, there were more than 5,700 people on the waiting list and only a handful of new fans are given the opportunity to buy season tickets each year.

How to Contact the Team about Tickets

24-hour touch-tone ticket ordering:
617-482-4769 (617-482-4SOX)
Online ordering: redsox.com
Ticket office at Fenway Park: 877-733-7699 (877-RED-SOX9)
Open Monday through Friday, 10 a.m. to 5 p.m.

If you have any questions about how to obtain tickets from the Red Sox, you can contact them in the following ways:

Mail: Boston Red Sox
         4 Yawkey Way
         Boston, MA
         02215-3496

Phone: 617-267-9440

To order tickets to accommodate fans with disabilities, call 877-733-7699.

Buying Tickets from Resellers

When fans aren't able to buy tickets from the team, or if they can't obtain the type of seats they desire, they often turn to resellers. To see many different tickets offered for sale for all the games, you can go to EBay, Stubhub.com or any number of different online ticket brokers. To find ticket brokers, just go to Google or Yahoo and search for "Red Sox tickets." Look carefully at the tickets offered at different ticket broker sites. You will usually find that many of them are offering the same exact tickets. This is because in order to increase their available inventory, ticket brokers pool their ticket listings to they can be displayed on many different sites. Usually the prices are the same from site to site, but often they are not.

There is no specific going rate for tickets, but in general you can obtain tickets at EBay or Stubhub.com for about double the ticket's face value. Prices from ticket brokers tend to start higher than that, and of course, the better the seats and the more desirable the game, the higher the markup.

If you want to go to a Yankee game at Fenway, the cost of buying from a reseller can be shocking. No matter which type of reseller you look at, you are likely to find prices starting at three to five times the face value.

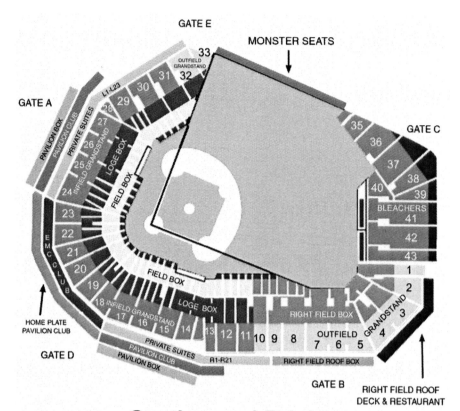

Seating and Pricing

Field Box	$105	**Green Monster**		
Loge Box	$85	Seats	$140	
Right Field Box	$45	Standing Room	$30	
Right Field Roof Box	$45	**Pavilion Level**		
Infield Grandstand	$45	EMC Club	$286	
Outfield Grandstand	$27	Home Plate Pavilion	$205	
Lower Bleachers	$23	Pavilion Club	$158	
Upper Bleachers	$12	Pavilion Box	$90	
Standing Room	$20	Standing Room	$25	
		Right Field Roof Restaurant	$110	
		Standing Room	$30	

Types of Seating

Infield Grandstand
Face value of tickets is $45

Comprised of sections 11-31, the Infield Grandstand sections are located directly behind the Loge Box sections and they run from the middle of the right field line (Section 11) to the middle of the left field line (Section 31), forming a horseshoe around the infield.

Along with the Outfield Grandstand sections, these seats can be affected by pole obstructions. For more information on the location of the poles, see the diagrams in the second half of this book. In general, Infield Grandstand seats are the best seats the average fan can expect to be able to buy from the team. This is because the vast majority of Loge Box and Field Box seats are sold to season ticket holders. There are standing room tickets available ($20) and hundreds of fans stand behind the Infield Grandstand sections during each game.

Outfield Grandstand
Face value of tickets is $27

Comprised of sections 1-10 and 32-33, the Outfield Grandstand sections are located next to the outer edges of the Infield Grandstand sections. The Outfield Grandstand sections located in right field (1-10) are some of the least sought after seats in the park due to their location and the odd way that many of the sections face center and left fields, rather than the infield. Sections 1 and 2 face the infield, but are extremely far from home plate. Sections 3 and 4 face the left field foul pole. Sections 5 though 10 are closer to home plate, but face left and center fields. If you sit in sections 5 through 10 you will spend most of the game looking to your left over the heads of hundreds of fans and it can be a pain in the neck, literally.

The sections in left field (32 and 33) are no alcohol, family sections. Seats in these two sections offer some of the best values in the park. The seats are close to the field and the Green Monster and they face the infield. These seats can be affected by pole obstructions. For more information on the location of the poles, see the diagrams in the second half of this book.

Loge Box
Face value of tickets is $85
The Loge Box sections are situated between the Grandstand and Field Box sections. They run from halfway down the right field line all the way around the infield until just before the Green Monster. Generally speaking, they offer a great view of the park.

The vast majority of these tickets are owned by season ticket holders. The Loge Box sections are in front of the poles, and only a handful of seats have any pole issues whatsoever.

One thing to keep in mind if you have the opportunity to buy Loge Box seats: the first two rows (AA and BB) can be affected by walkway traffic which can make it very difficult to enjoy the game. If possible, check to see if there is a walkway near the seats you are considering buying.

Field Box
Face value of tickets is $105
Field Box sections are located on the field from halfway down the right field line to halfway down the left field line. They are closer to the action than any other seats in the park and they are almost all owned by season ticket holders.

Infield Dugout Box, Extended Dugout Box, and Canvas Alley Dugout Box
Face value of tickets is $312 for Infield Dugout Box, $260 for Extended Dugout Box, and $130 for Canvas Alley Dugout Box
These are all super-premium seats added in the past several years. They are directly on the field, surrounding the infield and are in front of the field box seats. In most cases there are only two rows of these seats.

Right Field Box
Face value of tickets is $45
Right Field Box sections are located in front of Grandstand sections 1 through 10. The majority of these seats are very good as they are close to the field and are reasonably priced.

Lower Bleachers
Face value of tickets is $23
The bleachers are located in center field (sections 34-40) and right field (sections 41-43).

The vast majority of bleacher seats are classified as "Lower Bleachers." The bleachers have plusses and minuses. If you sit there you know you won't ever have to deal with a pole affecting your view. However, you are far from home plate and you are open to the elements, especially the sun and rain. If you get seats in Sections 40-43, you may want to get seats above the fifth row to avoid having to look through a metal screen that separates the bleachers from the bullpens. The bleachers seem to go up forever, so be assured that there is a great deal of difference in the view from bleacher row 7 vs. bleacher row 45.

Upper Bleachers
Face value of tickets is $12

The Upper Bleacher sections 36-43 are located in the last 5 to 10 rows of each of those sections, usually at least 40 rows up. The team introduced these lower-priced bleacher seats about 5 years ago as a way to offer some seats in the park at a very affordable level. The $12 price has held steady for several years. Not surprisingly, at this price and with a relatively small quantity available, they are some of the first tickets to be sold.

The Upper Bleacher seats are further from home plate than any other seats in the park, but being so high up, they often are treated to cool breezes on hot days.

Green Monster
Face value of tickets is $140

Introduced several years ago to a tremendous amount of fanfare, the Green Monster seats are some of the most expensive and highly sought after seats in the park. There are only about 275 Green Monster seats, and given the love Sox fans have for their famous green wall, it is easy to understand why they are so popular. The seats are only sold through the preseason ticket lottery that usually occurs in February. Go to redsox.com in January or February to enter the lottery. There are standing room tickets available for $30, and these are sold to winners of the ticket lottery as well.

EMC Club
Face value of tickets is $286

Opened in 2006, the EMC Club replaced the .406 Club. Unlike the .406 Club these seats directly behind home plate are open to the elements as the glass windows were removed over the winter. At $286 a ticket it is unlikely that the average fan will ever watch a game from the EMC Club unless someone gives him a ticket.

Home Plate Pavilion Club
Face value of tickets is $205
Located above the EMC Club, these exclusive seats are also sold to season ticket holders. Another new section for 2006, these seats provide a great view of the field, but the cost is prohibitive for the average fan.

State Street Pavilion Club
Face value of tickets is $158
These seats just above the first and third base lines are located in the spot where the seats used to be called infield roof box seats. Opened in 2006, they are excellent seats for viewing the game.

Pavilion Box
Face value of tickets is $90
These seats just above the first and third base lines are located above the State Street Pavilion Club seats. Opened in 2006, they are part of the revamping of the upper level that took place in the winter of 2005-2006. Standing room tickets for this section are available for $25.

Right Field Roof Box
Face value of tickets is $45
Perched above Outfield Grandstand sections 5-9, these open-air seats offer a sparkling view of the entire park at a reasonable price. They are also located next to the Right Field Roof Deck Restaurant, however, you cannot enter the Roof Deck Restaurant area with a ticket for it.

Right Field Roof Deck Restaurant
Face value of tickets is $110
Constructed several years ago on the roof above Outfield Grandstand sections 1 through 4, the Right Field Roof Deck

Restaurant has a full menu, but to eat at one of the home plate-shaped tables you must have tickets for them. The opportunity to buy those tickets is obtained through a lottery that is usually held in February or March. Go to redsox.com in January or February to enter the lottery. The tickets are sold by the table, so you must buy four tickets for $440. The price of each ticket also includes a $25 credit towards your food bill ($100 total credit). Standing room tickets for this area are available for $30, and these are also sold to the winners of the ticket lottery in February or March.

Getting There and Parking

Most people who don't live in Boston get to Fenway by either driving or taking the "T," which is the greater Boston subway system.

Driving to Fenway

Driving can be a challenge, with the heavy city traffic and the difficulty you may have finding Fenway if you aren't familiar with downtown Boston. If you do drive, there are many different approaches, but if you are coming from the north, west, or south of the city, it is a good idea to take the Mass Pike (I-90) East to Exit 18-Cambridge and then follow these directions:

♦ Exit at Cambridge tolls and proceeds towards Cambridge
♦ Turn right onto Storrow Drive East (don't go over the Charles River bridge into Cambridge)
♦ Continue on Storrow Drive and take the Kenmore exit
♦ After exiting, turn right onto Beacon Street and in a few blocks you will be in Kenmore Square. Take a left onto Brookline Avenue and when you go over the Mass Pike you will see Fenway Park and several parking lots.

If you don't mind a 15-minute walk to the park, you can keep it simple by staying on the Mass Pike and getting off at Exit 22-Prudential Center and park in the Prudential Center garage. It is a 1-mile walk from the garage to the park.

If you get lost while driving, try to find your way to Kenmore Square.

Parking

There are lots ringing the park on Brookline Avenue and Boylston Street, with the biggest lot being on Brookline Avenue next to Boston Beer Works. If you park within a 5-minute walk to the park, the fee is usually $25 to $35. Two lots that are very convenient to the park and usually have spaces at least 1 hour before the game are the McDonald's restaurant lot on the corner of Boylston and Jersey streets, and a lot that is steps away from the player's entrance and Gate D on the corner of Van Ness Street and Yawkey Way.

See the map on page 26 for the location of parking lots closest to Fenway Park.

Taking the T

If you take the T, you want to get to the Green Line and get off at the Kenmore stop. If you are on the D branch of the Green Line you can also get off at the Fenway stop. At either stop, it is only a few minutes walk to the park.

One common way to avoid driving all the way into Boston is to go to exit 22 on I-95/128 and park at the Riverside MBTA Station. From the north or south you can simply get off at that exit. From the west you can take the Mass Pike to the I-95/128 exit 14, then go south on I-95/128 for 1 mile until you get to exit 22.

There is a 925-space parking lot at the Riverside Station. The fee to park is $3.75 and the subway fare is $2 for adults and free for children 11 and under. If you get on the T at the Fenway station after the game the outbound trip is free. It is a 30-minute ride on the T from the Riverside Station to the Fenway or Kenmore station. For more information visit mbta.com or call 617-222-5000.

Taking the Fenway Tour

Touring Fenway makes a great addition to your visit to the park. The tours include access to areas that the average fan would ordinarily never see, such as the press box, and areas that can usually only be seen after buying an expensive and hard to get ticket, such as the Right Field Roof Deck Restaurant. Please be aware that the areas the tours visit vary based on what is happening in the park that day.

Tours are available 7 days a week all year long. They start hourly on Monday through Saturday from 9 a.m. to 4 p.m. and from noon to 4 p.m. on Sunday. To obtain tickets, go to the Souvenir Store on Yawkey Way, which is across the street from the main entrance to the park. The cost is $12 for adults and $10 for children and the tours last just about 1 hour.

On game days, the last tour begins 3 hours before the scheduled start time. The last tour of the day on game days is abbreviated, so if you are going to a 2 p.m. Sunday game or 7 p.m. night game it is recommended that you don't go on the last tour so you will be able to experience as much as possible.

In addition to learning a great deal about the park's history from the guides, some of the tour stops often include:
♦ Green Monster seats
♦ the press box
♦ the new Pavilion Club
♦ a walk around the entire field on the warning track, which gives you the opportunity to take pictures in front of the Green Monster
♦ the dugout

If you have tickets to a 7 p.m. game and you want to make a full day of your Fenway experience, here is a suggested itinerary:
♦ take the noon or 1 p.m. tour

- when the tour is over, go to Gate D to watch the players come in and give the kids a chance to get autographs (2 to 4 p.m.)
- go to dinner, see pages 26–32 for restaurant listings
- back to the park when the gates open at 5 p.m. to watch batting practice and settle in for the game

To contact the Red Sox regarding tours, call 617-226-6666, or email tours@redsox.com. You may want to call ahead to make sure the tour time you have selected has not been cancelled for that day. You can also obtain tour information at redsox.com/tours.

Restaurant and Bar Locator Map

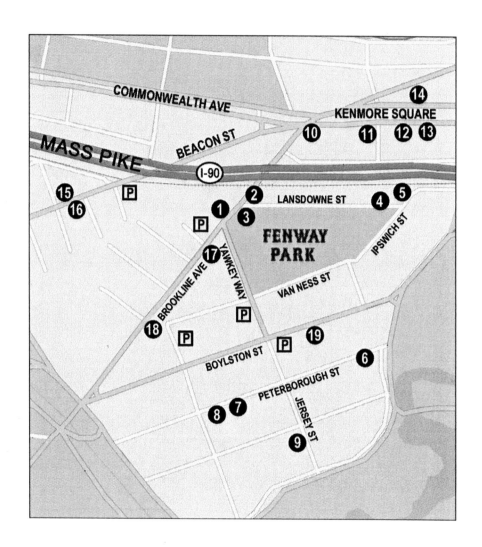

Restaurants near Fenway Park

1. Boston Beer Works
2. Cask'n'Flagon
3. Game On!
4. Tiki Room
5. Jillian's
6. Canestaro's Restaurant and Pizzeria
7. El Pelón Taqueria
8. Thornton's Fenway Grille
9. Brown Sugar Café
10. Pizzeria Uno
11. Great Bay
12. Ankara Café
13. India Quality
14. Bertucci's
15. Audubon Circle Restaurant and Bar

The Bar and Nightclub Scene

16. Au Tua Nua, 835 Beacon St., 617-262-2121
17. Copperfield's, 98 Brookline Ave. 617-247-8605
18. Boston Billiard Club, (55 pool tables)
    126 Brookline Ave., 617-536-7665
19. Baseball Tavern, 1270 Boylston St., 617-867-6526
1. Boston Beer Works, see page 28
2. Cask'n'Flagon, see page 28
3. Game On!, see page 29
4. Tiki Room, see page 29
5. Jillian's, see page 29

The following nightclubs and bars are all located on Lansdowne Street between the Cask'n'Flagon and Tiki Room.

Jake Ivory's (dueling pianos) 1 Lansdowne St., 617-247-1222
Tequila Rain, 7 Lansdowne St. 617-859-0030
Axis, 13 Lansdowne St., 617-262-2437
Avalon 15 Lansdowne St., 617-262-2424

P Parking lot

Restaurant listings are on pages 28-32

Where to Eat and Drink Before or After the Game

All of the restaurants listed in this section are less than a 10-minute walk to Fenway. They all have menus diverse enough for kids, but the restaurants closest to Fenway (less than a 5-minute walk) do get extremely crowded during the two hours before a game.

TIPS

♦ Visit the Web site and/or call the restaurant for more detailed information

♦ If driving, try to make sure you pick a parking lot that is on the same side of the park as where you plan to eat

♦ If you don't want a long wait for a table and enjoy a less crowded scene, pick a restaurant that is a 5 to 10 minute walk to the park

Boston Beer Works
61 Brookline Ave.   617-536-BEER   beerworks.net
walking distance to Fenway: 1 minute   map location: ❶
Just outside the park near Gate E, this lively and large restaurant and brewpub offers microbrews and a diverse menu to please any taste. If it's not too crowded (you'll often see long lines waiting to get in before a game) the variety and quality of the food makes it a good place for kids.

Cask'n Flagon
62 Brookline Ave.   617-536-4840   casknflagon.com
walking distance to Fenway: 1 minute   map location: ❷
Located across the street from Fenway near Gate E, this is the oldest and most famous sports bar in the area. Serves a full menu of appetizers, sandwiches, burgers, ribs, and steaks.

See Restaurant and Bar Locator Map on page 26

Game On!
82 Lansdowne St.   617-351-7001   gameonboston.com
walking distance to Fenway: 1 minute   map location: ❸
This is a big-time sports bar located inside Fenway Park, just
across the street from the Cask'n Flagon. You cannot enter the
game through the restaurant. It features 70 high-definition TVs
and its menu includes appetizers, salads, burgers, sandwiches,
and brick oven pizzas. The Heart Stopper Burger with crumbled
blue cheese and bacon is divine.

Tiki Room
1 Lansdowne St.   617-351-2580   tikiroomboston.com
walking distance to Fenway: 1 minute   map location: ❹
Fruity, exotic drinks, a faux tropical atmosphere, and interesting
platters for groups or families are what you will find at this spot
just past center field in the nightclub area of Lansdowne Street.

Jillian's
145 Ipswich St.   617-437-0300   jilliansboston.com
walking distance to Fenway: 1 minute   map location: ❺
A self-proclaimed "70,000 square foot food entertainment
universe," Jillian's is on the second floor of a three-story building
that includes a nightclub on the first floor, Tequila Rain, and
bowling on the third floor at Lucky Strike. Jillian's boasts
numerous pool tables and has a reasonably priced menu
(everything under $10) of appetizers, sandwiches, salads, and
pizzas. Located next to the Tiki Room.

See Restaurant and Bar Locator Map on page 26

Canestaro's Restaurant and Pizzeria
16 Peterborough St. 617-266-8997 canestaros.com
walking distance to Fenway: 8 minutes map location: **6**
This charming Italian restaurant and pizzeria is tucked away in a
quiet residential neighborhood a short walk from Fenway. It
serves outstanding Italian food and pizza at reasonable prices and
is a great spot for relaxing before or after a game.

El Pelón Taqueria
92 Peterborough St. 617-262-9090 elpelon.com
walking distance to Fenway: 7 minutes map location: **7**
Just want a quick bite? Stop by this authentic taqueria for a
quick, inexpensive, tasty burrito. Most meals are less than $5. No
beer available.

If you don't have time for a sit-down meal, there are plenty of carts on the
streets around the park serving up all kinds of hot sandwiches,
particularly on Lansdowne Street behind the Green Monster.

See Restaurant and Bar Locator Map on page 26

Thornton's Fenway Grille
100 Peterborough St.   617-421-0104
walking distance to Fenway: 7 minutes   map location: **8**
A lengthy, varied menu and relaxed sidewalk patio make this one of the better pre-game options within walking distance. Known for its casual atmosphere and friendly wait staff this is a great choice for any family or group.

Brown Sugar Cafe
129 Jersey St.   617-266-2928   brownsugarcafe.com
walking distance to Fenway: 6 minutes   map location: **9**
Considered by many to have the best Thai food in Boston, this charming spot has a diverse menu and a second location at 1033 Commonwealth Ave.

Pizzeria Uno
645 Beacon St.   617-262-4911   pizzeriauno.com
walking distance to Fenway: 4 minutes   map location: **10**
Deep-dish Chicago style pizza, a full Italian menu, and more await at this reliable chain restaurant.

Great Bay
500 Commonwealth Ave.   617-532-5300   greatbayrestaurant.com
walking distance to Fenway: 5 minutes   map location: **11**
Located in the Hotel Commonwealth in Kenmore Square, this first-class seafood restaurant opened in 2003 and has received rave reviews for its cuisine and ambience. Entrees are about $20 to $25 and reservations are recommended.

Ankara Cafe
472 Commonwealth Ave.   617-437-0404   ankaracafe.com   walking distance to Fenway: 6 minutes   map location: **12**
This tiny Turkish eatery in Kenmore Square offers authentic Mediterranean food for $5 to $8 a meal, and boasts more than 60 flavors of frozen yogurt. Definitely not fancy, but good, quick, and cheap.

See Restaurant and Bar Locator Map on page 26

India Quality
484 Commonwealth Ave.   617-267-4499
walking distance to Fenway: 6 minutes   map location: **13**
Located in Kenmore Square, one diner called this restaurant a
"hidden jewel in downtown Boston." It has received Zagat's Best
of Boston award for Indian food and has a large dining room.

Bertucci's
533 Commonwealth Avenue 617-236-1030 bertuccis.com walking
distance to Fenway: 6 minutes   map location: **14**
Brick-oven pizza with unusual toppings and delectable pasta,
seafood, and meat dishes await at this popular Italian chain
restaurant.

Audubon Circle Restaurant and Bar
838 Beacon St   617-421-1910
walking distance to Fenway: 10 minutes   Map location: **15**
A short walk down Beacon Street from Kenmore Square, the
Audubon has a trendy design and a great atmosphere. Far
enough from Fenway so that it won't be overwhelmed with fans
on game day, diners rave about the burgers and sandwiches.

See Restaurant and Bar Locator Map on page 26

Eating and Drinking in the Park

While the physical improvements and new seats in the park have garnered the most attention in recent years, the improvements to the quality and variety of food and beverages have probably had a greater impact on the average fan's experience. If you were sitting in Section 32, row 10 in 1999, and you sit there in 2007, your experience of watching the game has not changed much at all. However, your access to high quality food, beverages, and more comfortable areas to consume them has improved immeasurably.

It was only about 5 years ago when the fare inside Fenway was generally limited to hot dogs, sausage, french fries, and pretzels. For beer, you usually had to choose between Bud Light and Coors Light.

Fast forward to 2007 and your choices include Philly Cheesesteaks, El Tiante Cuban sandwiches, barbecued chicken, humongous hot dogs at RemDawg's on Yawkey Way, clam chowder, and more. Beer options include Sam Adams in several areas of the park, as well as Guinness, Harp, and Smithwick's, which are only available near section 19. Frozen margaritas and daiquiris are available near section 26.

Sushi will also be available beginning in 2007 to honor the arrival of Daisuke Matsuzaka from Japan.

Since late in the 2003 season the portion of Yawkey Way that runs from Gate A to Gate D has essentially become part of the ballpark for two hours prior to and during the entire game. The team received permission from the city of Boston to close that portion of the street off so that it can be used only by fans with tickets to the game. This means that more concessions are available to fans throughout the game, including El Tiante's and RemDawg's. It also means that fans have access to the huge souvenir store on Yawkey Way during the entire game.

The areas inside the park to buy and eat your food have also been improved dramatically. A couple of years ago the team cleared out some space in right field and behind the bleachers and created a huge open-air concourse for concessions, complete with picnic tables and TV monitors to watch the game. Similarly, the left field concession area has been expanded and includes several huge plasma TVs to watch the game while you wait for your food.

Fenway Park's concession vendor, Aramark, announced in March 2007 that oils used for cooking all fried food in the park will free of trans fats.

There are also new and improved concession areas on the Green Monster and in the Pavilion sections, but you must be ticketed for those sections to get in.

The Right Field Roof Deck Restaurant has a full menu, but to eat at one of the home plate-shaped tables you must have tickets for them. The opportunity to buy those tickets is obtained through a lottery that is usually held in February or March. Tickets are $110 each (sold only in sets of 4, so you get your own table for $440), and the price of each ticket includes $25 towards your food bill.

What all these improvements mean is that you no longer have to eat before you come into the game if you want a variety of tasty things to eat. If you want to enjoy the park when it is not crowded and catch batting practice, the gates open 2 hours prior to the scheduled start time.

36

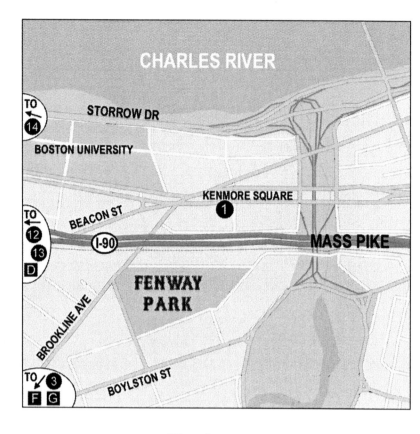

Hotels

1. Hotel Commonwealth
2. Eliot Hotel
3. Best Western Boston – The Inn at Longwood Medical
4. Hilton Boston Back Bay
5. Sheraton Boston
6. Marriott Boston Copley Place
7. Courtyard by Marriott Boston Copley Square
8. Lenox Hotel Boston
9. Colonnade Hotel
10. Westin Copley Place
11. Fairmont Copley Plaza
12. Holiday Inn Boston Brookline
13. Courtyard Boston Brookline
14. Doubletree Guest Suites Boston

Lodging listings are on pages 38-47

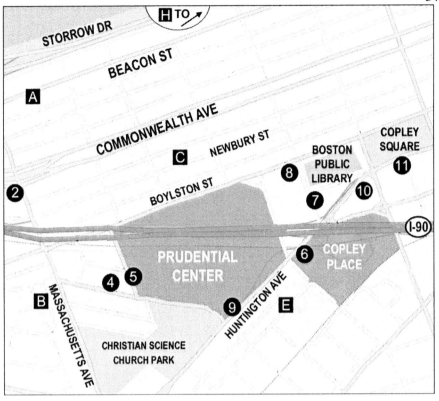

Bed and Breakfasts, Inns, and Guest Houses

A 463 Beacon Guest House
B Oasis Guest House
C Newbury Guest House
D Anthony's Town House
E Copley Inn
F Longwood Inn
G Beechtree Inn Bed & Breakfast
H The John Jeffries House

Lodging listings are on pages 38-47

Where to Stay

Boston hotels tend to be expensive, with rooms at 3-star or better hotels often averaging $200 to $350 per night. This section will list places to stay and their key information in two ways:

1. Hotels, beginning with those closest to Fenway Park
2. Bed and Breakfasts, Inns, and Guest Houses

Boston is a very popular business and tourist destination, and hotels fill up quickly. Having the Red Sox in town for a home game certainly adds to the scarcity of available rooms. You are advised to make your reservations early, as soon after you get your tickets as possible.

When considering a hotel or inn, you should check the availability and cost to park your car, and include that in your travel budget.

Keep in mind that the city of Brookline is literally just a few blocks from Fenway Park. Several of the hotels and inns listed in this section are in Brookline, as their location often makes them more convenient to Fenway than many downtown Boston hotels.

Staying Outside the City of Boston

Staying in one of the Boston suburbs, such as Newton, Braintree, or Dedham has the advantage of being generally less expensive and you will usually get free parking. If you don't want to drive into the city for the game, you should talk to the hotel about the best way to get to Fenway. Some hotels will offer a shuttle to the nearest T station.

See Lodging Locator Map on pages 36-37

Hotels listed by proximity to Fenway Park

(Two of the closest hotels to Fenway are the Hotel Buckminster in Kenmore Square and the Howard Johnson Fenway Park on Boylston Street. Due to the poor customer ratings these hotels received as of March 2007, they will not be listed in this section.)

Hotel Commonwealth
500 Commonwealth Ave.
617-933-5000
hotelcommonwealth.com

THE COUNT
★★★★
Distance to Fenway: ¼ mile
Rooms: 148
Pool: no
Fitness Center: yes
Average rate: $250-$350
Map location: ❶

Having just opened in 2003, this elegant hotel is the centerpiece of a revitalized Kenmore Square. The location is perfect, with many rooms looking out on the back of the Green Monster, and the park just a 5-minute walk away. The downside is that rooms can be pricey and they fill up fast.

The Eliot Hotel
3700 Commonwealth Ave.
617-267-1607
eliothotel.com

THE COUNT
★★★★
Distance to Fenway: ½ mile
Rooms: 95, including 79 suites
Pool: no
Fitness Center: yes*
Average rate: $275-$395
Map location: ❷

This elegant hotel was voted "Best Boutique Hotel" by Boston Magazine in 2006, and 79 of the 95 rooms are suites. The location is superb: less than a 10-minute walk from Fenway and a block from the shops on Newbury Street. It boasts the acclaimed Clio Restaurant, which serves innovative Asian-influenced French cuisine. Certainly a great destination for couples who can afford to treat themselves.

*There is no fitness center on site, but guests have access to the nearby Boston Sports Club

See Lodging Locator Map on pages 36-37

Best Western Boston – The Inn at Longwood Medical
342 Longwood Ave.
617-731-4700
bestwestern.com

THE COUNT
★★★
Distance to Fenway: ¾ mile
Rooms: 155
Pool: no
Fitness Center: yes
Average rate: $160-$220
Map location: **3**

Here you will find nicely appointed rooms, a friendly staff, and reasonable rates by Boston standards. However, unlike most hotels in this section, the Inn at Longwood is not within an easy walking distance of downtown Boston attractions. On the plus side, it is just off Brookline Avenue and is an easy 10-minute walk to Fenway.

Hilton Boston Back Bay
40 Dalton St.
617-236-1100
hilton.com

THE COUNT
★★★½
Distance to Fenway: 1 mile
Rooms: 385
Pool: indoor
Fitness Center: yes
Average rate: $225-$325
Map location: **4**

The Hilton offers what you would expect from an upscale hotel chain: clean, comfortable rooms, good service, and an indoor pool for the kids. A 15-minute walk to Fenway, this and the Sheraton are the closest of the cluster of hotels around the Prudential Center and Copley Square.

Sheraton Boston Hotel
39 Dalton St.
617-236-2000
sheraton.com/boston

THE COUNT
★★★★
Distance to Fenway: 1 mile
Rooms: 1216
Pool: indoor (with retractable roof)
Fitness Center: yes
Average rate: $250-$400
Map location: **5**

The largest of the hotels in the Prudential Center/Copley Square area, this hotel features an indoor pool with a retractable roof that opens in the summer. Connected to the Prudential Center mall.

See Lodging Locator Map on pages 36-37

Boston Marriott Copley Place
110 Huntington Ave.
617-236-5800
bostoncopleymarriott.com

THE COUNT
★★★★
Distance to Fenway: 1¼ miles
Rooms: 1100
Pool: indoor
Fitness Center: yes
Average rate: $250-$400
Map location: ❻

Situated next to the Prudential Center, there is an enclosed walkway that gets you to all the shops in the Prudential Center mall, a nice way to stay inside and cool on a hot summer day. The rooms are pricey, but the location, indoor pool, and Champions American Sports Bar in the lobby make it an attractive and comfortable place to stay.

Courtyard by Marriott Boston Copley Square
88 Exeter Ave.
617-437-9300
courtyardboston.com

THE COUNT
★★★
Distance to Fenway: 1¼ miles
Rooms: 81
Pool: no
Fitness Center: yes
Average rate: $225-$325
Map location: ❼

Across the street from the much larger Boston Marriott Copley Place, this boutique hotel is in a beautifully renovated building built in the late 1800s. Excellent location, and travelers enjoy the charm and uniqueness the rooms offer.

The Lenox Hotel Boston
710 Boylston St.
617- 536-5300
lenoxhotelboston.com

THE COUNT
★★★½
Distance to Fenway: 1¼ miles
Rooms: 212
Pool: no
Fitness Center: yes
Average rate: $200-$350
Map location: ❽

Located across the street from the Boston Public Library and a short walk from the Prudential Center and Copley Square, this charming hotel offers guest rooms that were beautifully renovated in 2005 and an Irish pub off the lobby.

See Lodging Locator Map on pages 36-37

The Colonnade Hotel
120 Huntington Ave.
617-424-7000
colonnadehotel.com

This European-style hotel gets high marks from travelers and boasts Boston's only rooftop pool, a great spot for summer sunset cocktails with views of the city.

THE COUNT
★ ★ ★ ★
Distance to Fenway: 1¼ miles
Rooms: 285
Pool: outdoor rooftop (summer)
Fitness Center: yes
Average rate: $150-$325
Map location: ❾

The Westin Copley Place
10 Huntington Ave.
617-262-9600
westin.com

Along with the Sheraton and the Marriott Copley, this is one of the three enormous hotels in the Copley/Prudential Center area, each with more than 800 rooms. Provides everything you would expect from an upscale hotel.

THE COUNT
★ ★ ★ ★
Distance to Fenway: 1¼ miles
Rooms: 803
Pool: indoor
Fitness Center: yes
Average rate: $195-$400
Map location: ❿

The Fairmont Copley Plaza
138 St. James Ave.
617-267-5300
fairmont.com/copleyplaza

Opened in 1912 (the same year as Fenway Park) and recently renovated, this stately and luxurious hotel is one of the crown jewels of Boston. A great choice for couples who want to treat themselves.

THE COUNT
★ ★ ★ ★
Distance to Fenway: 1½ miles
Rooms: 383
Pool: no
Fitness Center: yes
Average rate: $195-$400
Map location: ⓫

See Lodging Locator Map on pages 36-37

Holiday Inn Brookline Boston
1200 Beacon St., Brookline
617-277-1200
holidayinn.com

THE COUNT
★ ★ ★
Distance to Fenway: 1½ miles
Rooms: 383
Pool: indoor
Fitness Center: yes
Average rate: $140-$200
Map location: **12**

Renovated in 2004, this hotel is conveniently located on Beacon Street steps away from the St. Paul Street station of the T's Green Line. From there it is just 4 short stops to Kenmore. Reasonable by Boston standards – a good spot for families.

Courtyard Boston Brookline
40 Webster St., Brookline
617-734-1393
marriott.com

THE COUNT
★ ★ ★
Distance to Fenway: 1½ miles
Rooms: 193
Pool: indoor
Fitness Center: yes
Average rate: $160-$240
Map location: **13**

While technically located outside Boston in Brookline, this hotel near Coolidge Corner has a city feel to it. Fine restaurants and shops are just outside the door and the location near the T makes it very convenient.

Doubletree Guest Suites Boston
400 Soldiers Field Rd.
617-783-0090
doubletree.com

THE COUNT
★ ★ ★
Distance to Fenway: 2 miles
Rooms: 305, including 295 suites
Pool: indoor
Fitness Center: yes
Average rate: $169-$249
Map location: **14**

Located just off eastbound exit 18 on the Mass Pike, this virtually all-suite hotel is easy to find and a 5-minute drive to Fenway on Storrow Drive. While the suites, the price, and the indoor pool certainly make it attractive for families, keep in mind that it is not near a T station and the immediate vicinity is not conducive to stepping out and going to dinner or shopping. The hotel runs a free shuttle to Harvard Square, Copley, and Boston Common (but not to Kenmore).

See Lodging Locator Map on pages 36-37

Bed and Breakfasts, Inns, and Guest Houses

For those willing to depart from the predictable and usually reliable chain and large city hotels, a smaller establishment can offer a unique and memorable experience. To help ensure a pleasant stay, you are advised to do more research when booking a room at a B & B, inn, or guest house. If you reserve a room at a Marriott, for example, you can certainly make your reservation based solely on price and location: you generally know what you are going to get based on past experience at large chain hotels with good reputations. Just the opposite is true of small, family-run establishments. You should look at their Web site, read online traveler reviews at sites like tripadvisor.com, and call to speak with the owner or manager before reserving a room.

Be advised that since different travelers go into these rooms with different expectations, the opinions can vary greatly.

It is also true that Boston is one of the most historic cities in America, and many of these locations are housed in beautifully restored, century-old brownstone buildings. If you are going to Boston to bask in the history of America's greatest ballpark, why not extend that historical feel to your lodging?

Below are some common features that distinguish B&Bs, inns, and guest houses from large chain hotels. Some travelers may view some of these as positive attributes, and others just the opposite.

- ◆ there are usually only 10 to 30 rooms, so if it is a popular destination, call well in advance of your stay for reservations
- ◆ rooms at the same establishment often vary greatly in size and furnishings
- ◆ usually no pool or fitness room

See Lodging Locator Map on pages 36-37

- they are usually owned and run by families, and word-of-mouth advertising is very important to them, so they often do whatever they can to make you comfortable
- Guests often must share a bathroom (ask at time of booking)
- breakfast is often included (ask at time of booking)
- many require a 50% deposit or full-night's stay be paid at time of booking, and the cancellation policies are often different than traditional hotels (ask at time of booking)
- the uniqueness of a well-run and well-maintained small establishment will create many more lasting, positive memories than a typically forgettable stay at a large chain hotel.

463 Beacon Guest House
463 Beacon St.
617/536-1302
463beacon.com

THE COUNT
Distance to Fenway: ¾ mile
Rooms: 20
Average rate: $79-$149
Map location: **A**

The self-proclaimed "Boston's Best Slept Secret" is housed in a renovated brownstone in a great location just a short walk from Kenmore Square. The rooms vary greatly in shape and size, and sleep from one to four people. A good value.

Oasis Guest House
22 Edgerly Rd.
617-267-2662
oasisgh.com

THE COUNT
Distance to Fenway: ¾ mile
Rooms: 16
Average rate: $69-$100 for shared bath; $99-$150 for private bath
Map location: **B**

Located in a row of brownstones on a residential street, the Oasis is a short walk from Fenway Park and a multitude of shops and restaurants. Travelers give the friendly staff high marks, and guests can enjoy a cup of tea or cocktail on one of two small outdoor decks. The rooms are generally small, but very clean. Very well-liked by travelers.

See Lodging Locator Map on pages 36-37

Newbury Guest House
261 Newbury St.
617-437-0065
newburyguesthouse.com

An historic inn housed in what
used to be three Victorian homes,

THE COUNT
Distance to Fenway: 1 mile
Rooms: 32
Average rate: $110-$180
(breakfast included)
Map location: **C**

this charming inn has a great location and a lot of character.
Some travelers have said the photos on the Web site are
misleading.

Anthony's Town House
1085 Beacon St., Brookline
617-566-3972
anthonystownhouse.com

Housed in a beautifully restored
historic brownstone on Beacon

THE COUNT
Distance to Fenway: 1 mile
Rooms: 14
Average rate: $110-$150
Map location: **D**

Street, the rooms are decorated with French, Rococo, Venetian
and Victorian antiques. Travelers love the location and the
wonderful attitude of the owners. Call for information on large
rooms that could accommodate a family.

The Copley Inn
19 Garrison St.
617-236-0300
copleyinn.com

Housed in a brownstone on a
tree-lined street in the historic

THE COUNT
Distance to Fenway: 1 ¼ miles
Rooms: 20
Average rate: $135-$145
Map location: **E**

back bay neighborhood, this charming inn is just a short walk
from Copley Square and the T station. It offers good rates and a
great location, as well as a private bath and a kitchenette in each
room. Each room has exactly one queen bed, which makes it a
good choice for couples. Very well-liked by travelers.

See Lodging Locator Map on pages 36-37

Longwood Inn
123 Longwood Ave., Brookline
617-566-8615
longwood-inn.com

THE COUNT
Distance to Fenway: 1 ¼ miles
Rooms: 22
Average rate: $99-$129
Map location: **F**

This converted Victorian mansion in a residential neighborhood just three blocks from Boston includes rooms of varying sizes, a cozy, at-home atmosphere, and a friendly staff. One traveler said it "felt like being away at a cottage."

The Beechtree Inn Bed and Breakfast
83 Longwood Ave., Brookline
617-277-1620
thebeechtreeinn.com

THE COUNT
Distance to Fenway: 1 ¼ miles
Rooms: 10
Average rate: $89-$179
Map location: **G**

This quaint B &B is universally adored by travelers. The owner does an excellent job of making people feel at home and ensuring a positive stay. There are 10 distinct rooms of varying sizes and shapes, and you are able to view the exact room you will be reserving on the Web site.

The John Jeffries House
124 David G. Mugar Way
617-367-1866
johnjeffrieshouse.com

THE COUNT
Distance to Fenway: 2 miles
Rooms: 46
Average rate: $105-$175
Map location: **H**

This small hotel is further from Fenway than the other inns listed in this section, but it has many wonderful attributes: easy to find off Storrow Drive, a lot of rooms for an inn, a great location for exploring historic downtown Boston on foot, and a very charming and tasteful ambience. There are a variety of rooms and suites, so ask for specific information on your room before you book it, including the size and number of beds.

See Lodging Locator Map on pages 36-37

2004 Red Sox Postseason Quiz

This quiz will test your recollection of the most memorable month in the history of the Red Sox, October 2004. After completing the quiz, turn to page 54 for detailed answers.

1. Manny Ramirez held up a sign during the Red Sox World Series victory parade through Boston on October 30, 2004. What did it say?

A. I want to finish my career in Boston
B. I'm just Manny being Manny
C. Jeter is playing golf today
D. Thank you New England
E. Quo vadis, Nomar?

2. Which feeble, washed-up Yankee hurler served up a meatball to David Ortiz that he lined into the right field seats for a two-run, 1st-inning homer in Game 7 of the ALCS?

A. Tom Gordon
B. Randy Johnson
C. Mike Stanton
D. Kevin Brown
E. Mike Mussina

3. How many doubles did Trot Nixon hit in World Series Game 4?

A. 3
B. 1
C. none
D. 2
E. 4

See page 54 for answers to the quiz

4. Which Anaheim Angels slugger gave Sox fans agita by blasting a 7th-inning grand slam into the bullpen, tying the score of ALDS Game 3 at 6-6. Ultimately, it turned out to be a blessing, as it set up Big Papi's 10th-inning heroics.

A. Tim Salmon
B. David Eckstein
C. Doug DeCinces
D. Vladimir Guerrero
E. Garret Anderson

5. Complete the call uttered by Fox-TV analyst Tim McCarver after Big Papi won Game 5 of the ALCS with an RBI single to center in the 14th inning: "He didn't do it again, did he?..."

A. ... great googly-moogly!"
B. ... he's the man of the hour with a tower of power!"
C. ... yes, he did."
D. ... never has one man done so much for so many."
E. ... give me five, I'm still alive."

6. Which Red Sox pitcher set a major league record by recording wins in the deciding games in all three postseason series in the same year?

A. Pedro Martinez
B. Curt Schilling
C. Keith Foulke
D. Derek Lowe
E. Bronson Arroyo

See page 54 for answers to the quiz

7. Who did Keith Foulke strike out to end Game 6 of the ALCS?

A. Derek Jeter
B. Tony Clark
C. Jason Giambi
D. Alex Rodriguez
E. Jorge Posada

8. Which Red Sox player was struck in the head by a baseball thrown from the shore of the Charles River as the team floated by in Duck Boats during the World Series victory parade?

A. David Ortiz
B. Mark Bellhorn
C. Kevin Millar
D. Derek Lowe
E. Pedro Martinez

9. Game 4 of the 2004 ALCS was perhaps the most memorable game in Red Sox history. Who was the winning pitcher?

A. Keith Foulke
B. Alan Embree
C. Bronson Arroyo
D. Mike Timlin
E. Curtis Leskanic

10. Who hit a two-run homer in the 4th inning of ALDS Game 1 against Anaheim to put the Sox ahead 3-0 and send them on their way to an easy 9-3 triumph?

A. Kevin Millar
B. Manny Ramirez

See page 54 for answers to the quiz

C. David Ortiz
D. Johnny Damon
E. Mark Bellhorn

11. Which of the following headlines did NOT appear on a New York City newspaper on October 21, 2004, the day after the Sox won the ALCS in New York?

A. What a Choke!
B. Hell Freezes Over
C. Damned Yankees
D. Yankees Suck
E. The Choke's On Us

12. How many errors did the Red Sox commit in Games 1 and 2 of the World Series combined?

A. none
B. 8
C. 4
D. 1
E. 3

13. Who hit home runs in three consecutive postseason games?

A. Manny Ramirez
B. Mark Bellhorn
C. David Ortiz
D. Jason Varitek
E. Johnny Damon

See page 54 for answers to the quiz

52

14. Which overpaid Yankee superstar had only 1 hit in 17 at-bats and struck out 6 times in Games 4 through 7 of the ALCS?

A. Derek Jeter
B. Alex Rodriguez
C. Jorge Posada
D. Raul Mondesi
E. Gary Sheffield

15. Mark Bellhorn's game-winning two-run homer in the 8th inning of World Series Game 1 bounced off which fabled Fenway landmark?

A. The Green Monster
B. Dan Shaughnessy's ego
C. The Coke bottle above the Monster seats
D. Jerry Remy's mustache
E. The Pesky Pole

16. Who hit the memorable game-tying single up the middle past Mariano Rivera in the 9th inning of Game 4 of the ALCS?

A. Kevin Millar
B. David Ortiz
C. Bill Mueller
D. Dave Roberts
E. Trot Nixon

17. Which Red Sox pitcher started Game 1 of the World Series?

A. Pedro Martinez
B. Tim Wakefield
C. Curt Schilling

See page 54 for answers to the quiz

D. Bronson Arroyo
E. Derek Lowe

18. How many saves did Keith Foulke record in the World Series?

A. 3
B. 1
C. 4
D. none
E. 2

19. Which doctor performed an experimental procedure on Curt Schilling's ankle that enabled him to pitch (and win) Game 6 of the ALCS and Game 2 of the World Series?

A. Dr. James Andrews
B. Dr. Demento
C. Dr. Arthur Pappas
D. Dr. Pepper
E. Dr. Bill Morgan

20. Edgar Renteria hit a one-hopper that was "stabbed by Foulke" and underhanded to Doug Mientkiewicz at first to end the World Series. What uniform number was Renteria wearing?

A. 4
B. 11
C. 5
D. 24
E. 3

See page 54 for answers to the quiz

Answers to the Quiz

1. C	5. C	9. E	13. B	17. B
2. D	6. D	10. A	14. E	18. B
3. A	7. B	11. D	15. E	19. E
4. D	8. E	12. B	16. C	20. E

Detailed answers:

1. C. Jeter is playing golf today
A fan on the parade route handed the sign to Manny, and he happily displayed it throughout much of the rolling rally.

2. D. Kevin Brown
Brown was a horrible choice to start a deciding Game 7, having recently rejoined the team after breaking his hand punching a wall. But with games on 5 consecutive days, including 2 extra-inning classics, Joe Torre didn't have many options.

3. A. 3
Trot Nixon had a disappointing 2004 regular season. Hampered by injuries, he had only 149 at-bats. But the original Dirt Dog came through in the deciding game of the World Series, smacking three doubles and driving in two runs.

4. D. Vladimir Guerrero
Guerrero's dramatic 7th-inning grand slam was one of the only bright spots in the series for the prodigious slugger. Besides that hit, he was only 1 for 11.

5. C. ... yes, he did."
In terms of displaying a lack of enthusiasm when calling an exciting game, McCarver is surpassed in dullness only by his partner Joe Buck.

Quiz begins on page 48

6. D. Derek Lowe
Pitching in extra-inning relief, Lowe won Game 3 of the
Anaheim series. He then started and won Game 7 of the ALCS
and Game 4 of the World Series, pitching a total of 13 innings
and allowing only 1 run in those two games. Frustrated by being
left out of the starting rotation in the postseason, his availability
in key spots enabled him to become a postseason hero.

7. B. Tony Clark
The tying run was on base and Clark could have won the series
for the Yankees with a home run, but instead he waved helplessly
at a fastball high and away to end the game.

8. E. Pedro Martinez
Given Pedro's reputation as a "headhunter" on the mound,
perhaps some fans thought it appropriate that he take one off the
melon in one of his last acts as a Red Sox player.

9. E. Curtis Leskanic
Leskanic came into a two-out, bases-loaded jam in the top of the
11th inning and got Bernie Williams out on a fly to center. He
then pitched a scoreless top of the 12th, setting up Big Papi's
game-ending two-run blast in the bottom of the inning.

10. A. Kevin Millar
Millar didn't have too many memorable moments in the
postseason, and an early two-run homer in an eventual 9-3
blowout certainly isn't all that memorable. Those watching
closely, however, will always remember his walk in the 9th inning
of Game 4 in the ALCS that represented the tying run and
turned the series around.

11. D. Yankees Suck
While all five headlines are delightful and appropriate, it was
only Yankees Suck that the scribes from Gotham chose not to
use to commemorate the Yankees historic collapse.

Quiz begins on page 48

12. B. 8
Yes, the Red Sox committed 4 errors in Game 1 and 4 errors in Game 2 and still managed to win both games. Manny Ramirez made 2 errors in Game 1 and Bill Mueller made 3 in Game 2.

13. B. Mark Bellhorn
The diminutive second baseman hit a game-winning three-run homer in Game 6 of the ALCS, another solo shot in ALCS Game 7, and a game-winning two-run homer in Game 1 of the World Series. In the 2004 postseason, the Red Sox were truly Saved by the Bellhorn.

14. E. Gary Sheffield
While Sheffield was horrific at 1-17, his mates weren't much better: A-Rod was 2-17, Jeter was 4-19, and Posada was 4-17.

15. E. The Pesky Pole
Bellhorn's game-winner capped off the scoring in a wild 11-9 game. In the prior game at Yankee Stadium, Bellhorn also hit a homer off the right field foul pole.

16. C. Bill Mueller
The quiet, hard-working professional got the job done and came through with one of the biggest hits in team history.

17. B. Tim Wakefield
It was certainly appropriate that the honor of starting the first World Series game to be played in Fenway Park in 18 years go to Wakefield, the senior member of the team with 10 years of service at the time, and someone renowned for his hard work and selfless attitude.

18. B. 1
Foulke was stellar in the World Series, pitching a total of 5 innings, giving up only one run, while allowing four hits and one walk with 8 strikeouts. He recorded the last out of each of the

Quiz begins on page 48

four games, but only 1 save. He was the winning pitcher in Game 1, and Games 2 and 3 were non-save situations. His only save came in Game 4.

19. E. Dr. Bill Morgan

One of the great unsung heroes in Red Sox history, team doctor Bill Morgan practiced his experimental procedure on human cadaver legs before inserting several sutures into Schilling's ankle to help keep the tendon in place.

20. E. 3

Renteria wore the same number as Babe Ruth. The Curse of the Bambino, if you believe in it, was finally broken.

Quiz begins on page 48

WHO'S YOUR **PAPI?**

JETER DRINKS WINE COOLERS

LOOKS LIKE JESUS
THROWS LIKE MARY
ACTS LIKE JUDAS
JOHNNY BE GONE!

LOVE ME,
ORTIZ ME?

WORST CHOKE IN SPORTS HISTORY

The Rivalry with the Yankees

If you want to understand the intensity of the rivalry between the Red Sox and Yankees, all you need to do is consider the receptions given to departed Sox stars Pedro Martinez and Johnny Damon upon their returns to Fenway Park in 2006. Both players came back to Fenway in highly anticipated debuts as opposing players in the first half of the 2006 season. Pedro, returning as a pitcher for the New York Mets, was treated royally by the fans, cheered like the baseball god of Beantown he was for seven years. Damon, however, was booed unmercifully when he came back clean shaven and wearing the hated drab, gray uniform of the Evil Empire. It was then that Johnny may have realized what he sacrificed when he went to New York: if he stayed in Boston he would have been treated like a king forever as the man who almost single-handedly won Game 7 of the 2004 ALCS against the Yankees; but in the Bronx, if he doesn't win the World Series every year, he is just another overpaid bum.

The baseball life of a Red Sox fan for most of the twentieth century was defined by feeling inferior to the Yankees. And with good reason: from 1923 through 2000 the Yankees won 26 World Series titles while the Red Sox won zero. (Curse of the Bambino, Bucky Dent, Bill Buckner, etc. You know the stories).

But then in 2001 things began to gradually change to the delight of Sox fans everywhere. The Yankees, while seemingly having their fifth World Series title in six years all sewn up, lost in the ninth inning of Game 7 to the Arizona Diamondbacks. The loss was stunning and excruciating (for Yankee fans). With the best relief pitcher in the history of baseball on the mound, the Yankees coughed up the lead and lost on a walkoff bloop single to shortstop. The loss was, well, almost Soxian.

But things didn't get any better for Sox fans in 2003 when the team got into the playoffs for the first time in the new millennium. The 2003 ALCS against the Yankees was an exciting but ultimately devastating series for Sox fans. There was a brawl in Game 3 and Pedro tossed 72-year-old Yankees bench coach Don Zimmer to the ground. Game 7 was a bona fide horror show for Sox fans: manager Grady Little left Pedro in too long as he coughed up a 4-0 lead, and Aaron Boone hit a walkoff home run off Tim Wakefield in extra innings. People all over New England wanted to go to bed and not get up for about 6 months.

2004 was, of course, the greatest year in Sox history. The heroics of David Ortiz, Curt Schilling, Johnny Damon, and so many others are well chronicled. They vanquished their unvanquishable foe in the Yankees and did it in a way that no one will ever forget. Sox fans could finally shed their feelings of inferiority. And with good reason: as Jason Varitek said before the World Series victory parade in Boston, Sox fans can now walk into Yankee Stadium with their heads held high.

Following the 2004 season Yankee fans wallowed in utter humiliation. They didn't have much to say about the Sox and their fans. The unthinkable, unimaginable, and impossible had happened. As one New York tabloid headline read the day after the Yankees lost the ALCS to the Red Sox, *Hell Freezes Over*.

The high point for this generation of Yankees was the 2000

World Series championship. Winning 4 out of 5 titles and beating the Mets at the same time made the Yankees and their fans feel invincible. However, ever since 2000 the Yankee dynasty has been in steady decline. They lost postseason series to the Diamondbacks, Angels and Marlins from 2001-2003. In each series they held an advantage and managed to lose two or three consecutive games to end the series.

The Yankee fan, smug in his recent World Series success, could make excuses for each loss: 2001 against the Diamondbacks was bad luck, in 2002 they ran into some hot pitchers on Anaheim, and in 2003 David Wells got hurt in a key moment and Josh Beckett of the Marlins was unexpectedly dominant.

There is no explaining away what happened in 2004 and beyond.

The dynasty's steady decline quickly devolved into an all-out free fall. After going up 3 games to none on the Red Sox, the Yankees are 3-10 in their last 13 postseason games from 2004-2006, having lost three consecutive series. This is an astonishing fall from grace for a franchise that was 33-8 in postseason games from 1998-2000.

The Yankee Magic has officially left the building. The pixie dust has all been blown away by the majestic swings of a smiling Dominican DH and the indomitable spirit of a man who wore a blood red sock. The Yankees are now the Enron of baseball, a bloated corpse on the beach.

Things have been decidedly different between the rivals since the new owners, led by John Henry and Tom Werner, took over early in 2002. The Red Sox were often a very good team, but usually a notch or two below the Yankees. And of course, they could never win the big game. The new owners and management have fostered a culture around the team that says we can compete at the same level as the Yankees. The team has shown a willingness to spend significant money on proven winners like Curt Schilling while simultaneously developing a strong farm system that has produced outstanding young pitchers like Jonathan Papelbon and Jon Lester.

In fact, since 2002 the Red Sox have a postseason record of 17-12. During that same span the Yankees have a very unYankeelike postseason record of 19-22.

The most telling example of the Red Sox desire to be better than the Yankees is the record $51.1 million fee the team paid for the rights to negotiate a contract with 26-year-old pitcher Daisuke Matsuzaka of Japan in November 2006. Intent on keeping Matsuzaka out of a Yankee uniform, the Red Sox winning bid was $19 million more than the Yankees.

What does all this mean to fans who want to go see the Yankees play the Sox at Fenway? The games are much more intense, the energy in the park is much higher than usual, and tickets are much harder to come by. Your best shot at getting tickets for a reasonable cost is to either win the ticket purchasing opportunity lottery or find a friend or business associate who can get you tickets. Other than that, you can expect to pay, pay, pay for the privilege of watching the greatest rivalry in sports.

Understanding the Seating Diagrams

		1	2	3	4	5	6	7	8	9	10	11	12
R	**10**	1	2	3	4	5	6	7	8	9	10	11	12
O	**9**	1	2	3	4	5	6	7	8	9	10	11	12
W	**8**	1	2	3	4	5	6	7	8	9	10	11	12
	7	1	2	3	4	5	6	7	8	9	10	11	12
	6	1	2	3	4	5	6	7	8	9	10	11	12
	5	1	2	3	4	5	6	7	8	9	10	11	12
	4	1	2	3	4	5	6	7	8	9	10	11	12
	3	1	2	3	4	5	6	7	8	9	10	11	12
	2	1	2	3	4	5	6	7	8	9	10	11	12
	1	1	2	3	4	5	6	7	8	9	10	11	12

Detail of Section 12 Seating Diagram
Bold numbers running vertically are row numbers
Numbers in boxes running horizontally are seat numbers

The seating diagrams in this book are intended to help you identify the seats in Grandstand sections that have **a pole impeding your view of home plate, the pitcher's mound, or both.**

As you can see in this detail from Section 12, the shaded areas cover seats that have a pole between them and either home plate or the pitcher's mound. In this case, the shaded area on the right has a home plate obstruction, and the shaded area on the left has a pitcher's mound obstruction.

So, if you sit in Section 12, Row 7, Seat 7 you will have difficulty seeing home plate without having to move forward, backward, or side to side. Similarly, if you sit in Row 4, Seat 6 you will have difficulty seeing the pitcher's mound.

Many seat numbers are partially shaded. This means that the pole issues affecting that seat are not as intrusive as seats that are completely shaded. If you're not sure if a seat will have any pole issues by looking at the diagrams, it would be a good idea to pick seats that are at least 2 completely non-shaded seats away from the obstructed area.

Generally, the further back you are in a section, the less of a problem the pole will be for your view. The closer you are to a pole, the bigger it looks.

Section 1

Outfield Grandstand
Face Value of tickets is $27

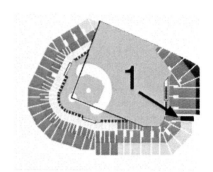

Section 1 is in right field behind
Right Field Box 87.

Section 1 borders the bleacher
seats, and the main difference
between sitting in Section 1 or
rows 15–30 of Bleacher Section 43 is that Section 1 is covered by
a roof in case it rains. With only 8 seats in each row, it does
make the seats feel less congested than most other sections and
you have easier access to the seats. Also, unlike many of the other
Outfield Grandstand sections, these seats face home plate, and
not left field.

There is a pole near row 1, seat 1 that affects that seat and one or
two others in each row running diagonally up to row 17, seat 5.

The view from the center of Section 1

Section I

ROW										ROW
18	1	2	3	4						18
17	1	2	3	4	5	6	7	8		17
16	1	2	3	4	5	6	7	8		16
15	1	2	3	4	5	6	7	8		15
14	1	2	3	4	5	6	7	8		14
13	1	2	3	4	5	6	7	8		13
12	1	2	3	4	5	6	7	8		12
11	1	2	3	4	5	6	7	8		11
10	1	2	3	4	5	6	7	8		10
9	1	2	3	4	5	6	7	8		9
8	1	2	3	4	5	6	7	8		8
7	1	2	3	4	5	6	7	8		7
6	1	2	3	4	5	6	7	8		6
5	1	2	3	4	5	6	7	8		5
4	1	2	3	4	5	6	7	8		4
3	1	2	3	4	5	6	7	8		3
2	1	2	3	4	5	6	7	8		2
1	1	2	3	4	5	6	7	8		1

 = View of home plate or pitcher's mound is obstructed

home plate

Section 2

Outfield Grandstand
Face Value of tickets is $27

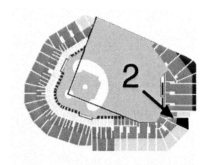

Section 2 is in right field behind
Right Field Box 88.

Section 2 is a large section in
right field that is far from home
plate. Unlike many of the other
Outfield Grandstand sections, these seats face home plate, and
not left field.

If you are facing the field, pole issues are limited to some seats on
the left side of the section. Any seat numbered 1 through 18 is
free from poles.

The view from the center of Section 2

Section 2

ROW

15 14 13 12 11 10 9 8 7 6 5 4 3 2 1

ROW	Seats
15	1 2 3 4 5 6 7 8 9 10 11 12 13 14 15 16 17 18 19 20 21 22 23 24 25 26 27 28 29
14	1 2 3 4 5 6 7 8 9 10 11 12 13 14 15 16 17 18 19 20 21 22 23 24 25 26 27 28
13	1 2 3 4 5 6 7 8 9 10 11 12 13 14 15 16 17 18 19 20 21 22 23 24 25 26 27
12	1 2 3 4 5 6 7 8 9 10 11 12 13 14 15 16 17 18 19 20 21 22 23 24 25 26 27
11	1 2 3 4 5 6 7 8 9 10 11 12 13 14 15 16 17 18 19 20 21 22 23 24 25 26
10	1 2 3 4 5 6 7 8 9 10 11 12 13 14 15 16 17 18 19 20 21 22 23 24 25
9	1 2 3 4 5 6 7 8 9 10 11 12 13 14 15 16 17 18 19 20 21 22 23 24 25
8	1 2 3 4 5 6 7 8 9 10 11 12 13 14 15 16 17 18 19 20 21 22 23 24
7	1 2 3 4 5 6 7 8 9 10 11 12 13 14 15 16 17 18 19 20 21 22 23 24
6	1 2 3 4 5 6 7 8 9 10 11 12 13 14 15 16 17 18 19 20 21 22 23
5	1 2 3 4 5 6 7 8 9 10 11 12 13 14 15 16 17 18 19 20 21 22
4	1 2 3 4 5 6 7 8 9 10 11 12 13 14 15 16 17 18 19 20 21 22
3	1 2 3 4 5 6 7 8 9 10 11 12 13 14 15 16 17 18 19 20 21
2	1 2 3 4 5 6 7 8 9 10 11 12 13 14 15 16 17 18 19 20
1	1 2 3 4 5 6 7 8 9 10 11 12 13 14 15 16 17 18 19

ROW

15 14 13 12 11 10 9 8 7 6 5 4 3 2 1

= View of home plate or pitcher's mound is obstructed

home plate →

Section 3

Outfield Grandstand
Face Value of tickets is $27

Section 3 is in right field behind
Right Field Box 89.

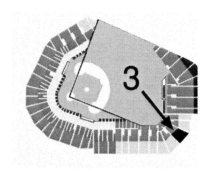

Section 3 is a large section
directly down the right field line
that is far from home plate.
Unlike many of the other Outfield Grandstand sections, these
seats face the infield, and not left field.

If you are facing the field, pole issues are limited to some seats on
the left side of the section. Beginning in row 4, seat 25, the
obstruction affects some seats up to row 15, seat 25. All the seats
in rows 1 through 3 are safe from poles, as well as any seats
numbered 1 through 22 in the entire section.

The view from the center of Section 3

Section 3

home plate

ROW
15 14 13 12 11 10 9 8 7 6 5 4 3 2 1

= View of home plate or pitcher's mound is obstructed

Section 4

Outfield Grandstand
Face Value of tickets is $27

Section 4 is in right field behind
Right Field Box 90.

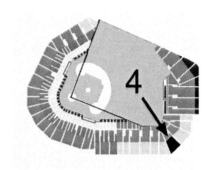

Tucked away in the right field
corner, seats in this section are
very far from home plate and
they face the left field foul pole, rather than the infield, which
causes you to have to look to the left to see the action. Although
they are fairly priced at $27, these are not very good seats.

There is a pole that affects seats 26 and 27 in the second row,
and the obstruction runs diagonally up through the section to
seats 19 and 20 in row 17.

The view from the center of Section 4

Section 4

home plate

= View of home plate or pitcher's mound is obstructed

Section 5

Outfield Grandstand
Face Value of tickets is $27

Section 5 is in right field behind
Right Field Box 91.

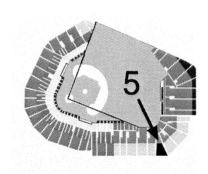

Tucked away in the right field
corner, seats in this section are
very far from home plate and
they face the Green Monster,
rather than the infield, which causes you to have to look to the
left to see the action. Although they are fairly priced at $27, these
are some of the worst seats in Fenway.

There is a pole obstruction that runs diagonally across the
section from the last few seats in row 3 to the first few seats in
row 9. All seats in rows 1, 2, and 10-17 are free from pole issues.

The view from the center of Section 5

Section 5

R O W

Seating chart (rows 17 down to 1; seat numbers increase toward home plate):

ROW	Seats
17	1 2 3 4 5 6 7 8 9 10 11 12 13 14 15 16 17 18 19 20 21 22 23 24 25 26 27 28 29 30
16	1 2 3 4 5 6 7 8 9 10 11 12 13 14 15 16 17 18 19 20 21 22 23 24 25 26 27 28 29 30
15	1 2 3 4 5 6 7 8 9 10 11 12 13 14 15 16 17 18 19 20 21 22 23 24 25 26 27 28 29
14	1 2 3 4 5 6 7 8 9 10 11 12 13 14 15 16 17 18 19 20 21 22 23 24 25 26 27 28
13	1 2 3 4 5 6 7 8 9 10 11 12 13 14 15 16 17 18 19 20 21 22 23 24 25 26 27
12	1 2 3 4 5 6 7 8 9 10 11 12 13 14 15 16 17 18 19 20 21 22 23 24 25 26 27
11	1 2 3 4 5 6 7 8 9 10 11 12 13 14 15 16 17 18 19 20 21 22 23 24 25 26
10	1 2 3 4 5 6 7 8 9 10 11 12 13 14 15 16 17 18 19 20 21 22 23 24 25
9	1 2 3 4 5 6 7 8 9 10 11 12 13 14 15 16 17 18 19 20 21 22 23 24 25
8	1 2 3 4 5 6 7 8 9 10 11 12 13 14 15 16 17 18 19 20 21 22 23 24
7	1 2 3 4 5 6 7 8 9 10 11 12 13 14 15 16 17 18 19 20 21 22 23
6	1 2 3 4 5 6 7 8 9 10 11 12 13 14 15 16 17 18 19 20 21 22 23
5	1 2 3 4 5 6 7 8 9 10 11 12 13 14 15 16 17 18 19 20 21 22
4	1 2 3 4 5 6 7 8 9 10 11 12 13 14 15 16 17 18 19 20 21
3	1 2 3 4 5 6 7 8 9 10 11 12 13 14 15 16 17 18 19 20
2	1 2 3 4 5 6 7 8 9 10 11 12 13 14 15 16 17 18 19 20
1	1 2 3 4 5 6 7 8 9 10 11 12 13 14 15 16 17 18 19

R O W

→ home plate

= View of home plate or pitcher's mound is obstructed

Section 6

Outfield Grandstand
Face Value of tickets is $27

Section 6 is in right field behind
Right Field Box 92.

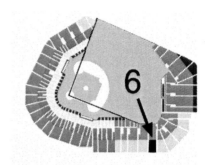

Tucked away in the right field
corner, seats in this section are
far from home plate and they
face center field, rather than the infield, which causes you to
have to look to the left to see the action. Compared to most
other sections in the park, these are not very good seats.

There is a pole obstruction that runs from the last few seats in
rows 4 and 5 diagonally across the section to the first seat in row
12. All seats in rows 1-3 and 13-17 are free from pole issues.

The view from the center of Section 6

Section 6

ROW	1	2	3	4	5	6	7	8	9	10	11	12	13	14	15	16	17	18	19	20	21	ROW
17	1	2	3	4	5	6	7	8	9	10	11	12	13	14	15	16	17	18	19	20	21	17
16	1	2	3	4	5	6	7	8	9	10	11	12	13	14	15	16	17	18	19	20	21	16
15	1	2	3	4	5	6	7	8	9	10	11	12	13	14	15	16	17	18	19	20	21	15
14	1	2	3	4	5	6	7	8	9	10	11	12	13	14	15	16	17	18	19	20	21	14
13	1	2	3	4	5	6	7	8	9	10	11	12	13	14	15	16	17	18	19	20	21	13
12	1	2	3	4	5	6	7	8	9	10	11	12	13	14	15	16	17	18	19	20	21	12
11	1	2	3	4	5	6	7	8	9	10	11	12	13	14	15	16	17	18	19	20	21	11
10	1	2	3	4	5	6	7	8	9	10	11	12	13	14	15	16	17	18	19	20	21	10
9	1	2	3	4	5	6	7	8	9	10	11	12	13	14	15	16	17	18	19	20	21	9
8	1	2	3	4	5	6	7	8	9	10	11	12	13	14	15	16	17	18	19	20	21	8
7	1	2	3	4	5	6	7	8	9	10	11	12	13	14	15	16	17	18	19	20	21	7
6	1	2	3	4	5	6	7	8	9	10	11	12	13	14	15	16	17	18	19	20	21	6
5	1	2	3	4	5	6	7	8	9	10	11	12	13	14	15	16	17	18	19	20	21	5
4	1	2	3	4	5	6	7	8	9	10	11	12	13	14	15	16	17	18	19	20	21	4
3	1	2	3	4	5	6	7	8	9	10	11	12	13	14	15	16	17	18	19	20	21	3
2	1	2	3	4	5	6	7	8	9	10	11	12	13	14	15	16	17	18	19	20	21	2
1	1	2	3	4	5	6	7	8	9	10	11	12	13	14	15	16	17	18	19	20	21	1

 = View of home plate or pitcher's mound is obstructed

home plate

Section 7

Outfield Grandstand
Face Value of tickets is $27

Section 7 is in right field behind
Right Field Box 93.

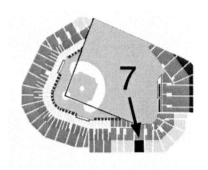

Located down the right field line
past the foul pole, seats in this
section are far from home plate
and they face left field, rather than the infield, which causes you
to have to look to the left to see the action. Compared to most
other sections in the park, these are not very good seats.

There are two pole obstructions in this section, one that affects
the first few rows in the lower-numbered seats, and one that runs
diagonally across the middle rows.

The view from the center of Section 7

Section 7

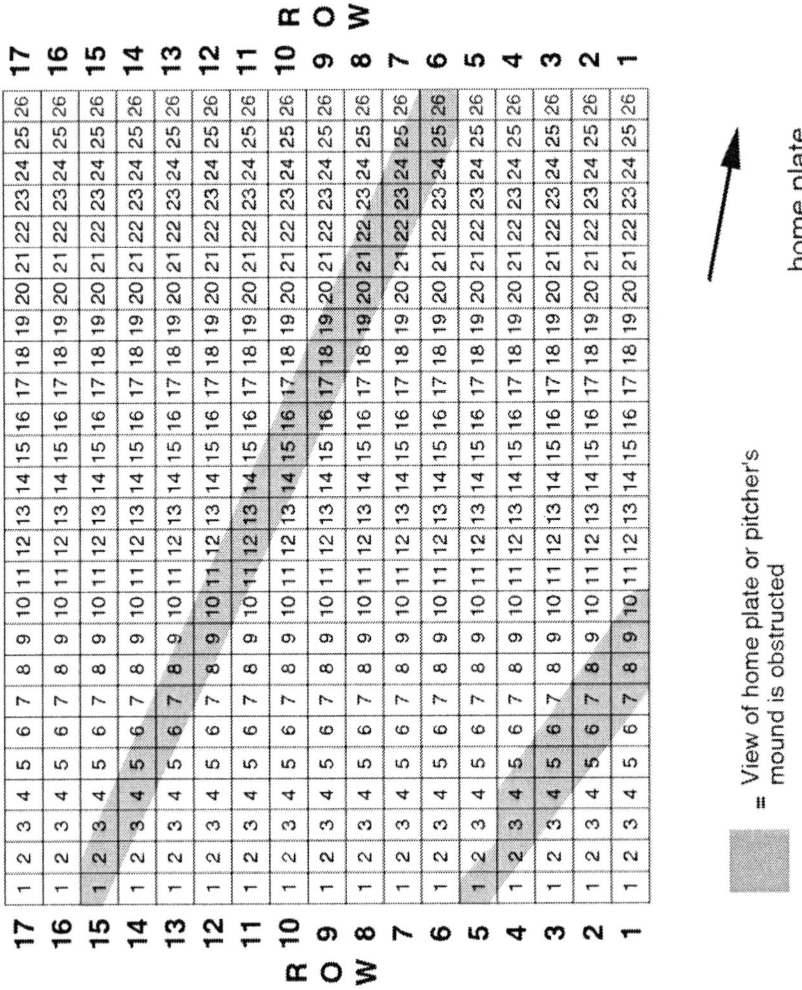

ROW

17 16 15 14 13 12 11 10 9 8 7 6 5 4 3 2 1

ROW

17 16 15 14 13 12 11 10 9 8 7 6 5 4 3 2 1

home plate

= View of home plate or pitcher's mound is obstructed

Section 8

Outfield Grandstand
Face Value of tickets is $27

Section 8 is in right field behind
Right Field Box 94.

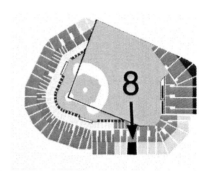

Located down the right field line
near the foul pole, seats in this
section face left field, rather than
the infield, which causes you to have to look to the left to see the
action.

There are two pole obstructions in this section, one that affects
the first few rows in the lower-numbered seats, and one that runs
diagonally across rows 7 through 17.

The view from the center of Section 8

Section 8

home plate

= View of home plate or pitcher's mound is obstructed

Section 9

Outfield Grandstand
Face Value of tickets is $27

Section 9 is in right field behind
Right Field Box 95.

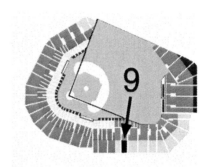

Located down the right field
line, seats in this section face left
field, rather than the infield,
which causes you to have to look to the left to see the action.

There are two pole obstructions in this section, one that affects
some seats in rows 1 through 7, and another that affects some
seats in rows 14 through 17. All seats in rows 8 through 13 are
free from pole issues.

The view from the center of Section 9

Section 9

17	1	2	3	4	5	6	7	8	9	10	11	12	13	14	15	16	17
16	1	2	3	4	5	6	7	8	9	10	11	12	13	14	15	16	16
15	1	2	3	4	5	6	7	8	9	10	11	12	13	14	15	16	15
14	1	2	3	4	5	6	7	8	9	10	11	12	13	14	15	16	14
13	1	2	3	4	5	6	7	8	9	10	11	12	13	14	15	16	13
12	1	2	3	4	5	6	7	8	9	10	11	12	13	14	15	16	12
11	1	2	3	4	5	6	7	8	9	10	11	12	13	14	15	16	11
R 10	1	2	3	4	5	6	7	8	9	10	11	12	13	14	15	16	10 R
O 9	1	2	3	4	5	6	7	8	9	10	11	12	13	14	15	16	9 O
W 8	1	2	3	4	5	6	7	8	9	10	11	12	13	14	15	16	8 W
7	1	2	3	4	5	6	7	8	9	10	11	12	13	14	15	16	7
6	1	2	3	4	5	6	7	8	9	10	11	12	13	14	15	16	6
5	1	2	3	4	5	6	7	8	9	10	11	12	13	14	15	16	5
4	1	2	3	4	5	6	7	8	9	10	11	12	13	14	15	16	4
3	1	2	3	4	5	6	7	8	9	10	11	12	13	14	15	16	3
2	1	2	3	4	5	6	7	8	9	10	11	12	13	14	15	16	2
1	1	2	3	4	5	6	7	8	9	10	11	12	13	14	15	16	1

 = View of home plate or pitcher's mound is obstructed

home plate

Section 10

Outfield Grandstand
Face Value of tickets is $27

Section 10 is in right field
behind Right Field Box 97.

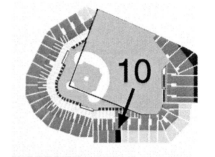

Located down the right field
line, this section is closer to the
infield than any other leftfield
grandstand section. The seats in neighboring Section 11 have a
face value of $45.

There is one obstruction in this section, beginning with the last
seat in row 5 moving diagonally to the first seat in row 11. All
seats in rows 1-4 and 12-17 are free from poles.

The view from the center of Section 10

Section 10

Rows 1–17, seats 1–13.

= View of home plate or pitcher's mound is obstructed

home plate

Section 11

Infield Grandstand
Face Value of tickets is $45

Section 11 is down the right
field line behind Loge Box
sections 98-100 and Field Box
sections 9-10.

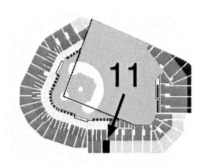

Section 11 borders Outfield
Grandstand Section 10, where tickets have a face value of $27.
This means that Section 11 is farther away from home plate than
any other Infield Grandstand section on the first base side, and
seats in Section 11 are much closer to the Pesky Pole than they
are to first base.

Pole issues in Section 11 are fairly mild. If you are seated
anywhere in the middle of the section you will have a clear view.

The view from the center of Section 11

Section II

ROW	1	2	3	4	5	6	7	8	9	10	11	12	13	14	15	16	17	18	19	20	ROW
17	1	2	3	4	5	6	7	8	9	10	11	12	13	14	15	16	17	18	19	20	17
16	1	2	3	4	5	6	7	8	9	10	11	12	13	14	15	16	17	18	19	20	16
15	1	2	3	4	5	6	7	8	9	10	11	12	13	14	15	16	17	18	19	20	15
14	1	2	3	4	5	6	7	8	9	10	11	12	13	14	15	16	17	18	19	20	14
13	1	2	3	4	5	6	7	8	9	10	11	12	13	14	15	16	17	18	19	20	13
12	1	2	3	4	5	6	7	8	9	10	11	12	13	14	15	16	17	18	19	20	12
11	1	2	3	4	5	6	7	8	9	10	11	12	13	14	15	16	17	18	19	20	11
10	1	2	3	4	5	6	7	8	9	10	11	12	13	14	15	16	17	18	19	20	10
9	1	2	3	4	5	6	7	8	9	10	11	12	13	14	15	16	17	18	19	20	9
8	1	2	3	4	5	6	7	8	9	10	11	12	13	14	15	16	17	18	19	20	8
7	1	2	3	4	5	6	7	8	9	10	11	12	13	14	15	16	17	18	19	20	7
6	1	2	3	4	5	6	7	8	9	10	11	12	13	14	15	16	17	18	19	20	6
5	1	2	3	4	5	6	7	8	9	10	11	12	13	14	15	16	17	18	19	20	5
4	1	2	3	4	5	6	7	8	9	10	11	12	13	14	15	16	17	18	19	20	4
3	1	2	3	4	5	6	7	8	9	10	11	12	13	14	15	16	17	18	19	20	3
2	1	2	3	4	5	6	7	8	9	10	11	12	13	14	15	16	17	18	19	20	2
1	1	2	3	4	5	6	7	8	9	10	11	12	13	14	15	16	17	18	19	20	1

= View of home plate or pitcher's mound is obstructed

home plate

Section 12

Infield Grandstand
Face Value of tickets is $45

Section 12 is down the right field
line behind Loge Box sections
101-104 and Field Box sections
11-15.

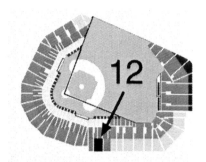

Pole issues in Section 12 are
confined to the right side of the section if you are facing the
field. Any seat with a number of 15 or higher is safe from poles.

The view from the center of Section 12

Section 12

17 | 1 2 3 4 5 6 7 8 9 10 11 12 13 14 15 16 17 18 19 20 21 22 23 24 | **17**

16 | 1 2 3 4 5 6 7 8 9 10 11 12 13 14 15 16 17 18 19 20 21 22 23 24 25 | **16**

15 | 1 2 3 4 5 6 7 8 9 10 11 12 13 14 15 16 17 18 19 20 21 22 23 24 25 | **15**

14 | 1 2 3 4 5 6 7 8 9 10 11 12 13 14 15 16 17 18 19 20 21 22 23 24 25 | **14**

13 | 1 2 3 4 5 6 7 8 9 10 11 12 13 14 15 16 17 18 19 20 21 22 23 24 25 | **13**

12 | 1 2 3 4 5 6 7 8 9 10 11 12 13 14 15 16 17 18 19 20 21 22 23 24 25 | **12**

11 | 1 2 3 4 5 6 7 8 9 10 11 12 13 14 15 16 17 18 19 20 21 22 23 24 25 | **11**

R
O   **10** | 1 2 3 4 5 6 7 8 9 10 11 12 13 14 15 16 17 18 19 20 21 22 23 24 25 | **10**   R
W   O
9 | 1 2 3 4 5 6 7 8 9 10 11 12 13 14 15 16 17 18 19 20 21 22 23 24 25 | **9**   W

8 | 1 2 3 4 5 6 7 8 9 10 11 12 13 14 15 16 17 18 19 20 21 22 23 24 25 | **8**

7 | 1 2 3 4 5 6 7 8 9 10 11 12 13 14 15 16 17 18 19 20 21 22 23 24 25 | **7**

6 | 1 2 3 4 5 6 7 8 9 10 11 12 13 14 15 16 17 18 19 20 21 22 23 24 25 | **6**

5 | 1 2 3 4 5 6 7 8 9 10 11 12 13 14 15 16 17 18 19 20 21 22 23 24 25 | **5**

4 | 1 2 3 4 5 6 7 8 9 10 11 12 13 14 15 16 17 18 19 20 21 22 23 24 25 | **4**

3 | 1 2 3 4 5 6 7 8 9 10 11 12 13 14 15 16 17 18 19 20 21 22 23 24 25 | **3**

2 | 1 2 3 4 5 6 7 8 9 10 11 12 13 14 15 16 17 18 19 20 21 22 23 24 25 | **2**

1 | 1 2 3 4 5 6 7 8 9 10 11 12 13 14 15 16 17 18 19 20 21 22 23 24 25 | **1**

= View of home plate or pitcher's mound is obstructed

home plate

Section 13

Infield Grandstand
Face Value of tickets is $45

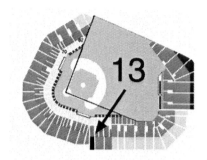

Section 13 is down the first base
line behind Loge Box section 105
and Field Box section 19.

Of all 33 Grandstand sections, 13
is one of the two smallest. Only
12 seats wide on the bottom, it gradually narrows to 6 seats in
the last 4 rows.

Pole issues in Section 13 run right down the middle of the
section. If you are sitting in the middle of the section you will see
a pole between home plate and the pitcher's mound. If you are
sitting on the left or right side of the section, there is a good
chance you will have a problem with a pole.

The view from the center of Section 13

Section 13

ROW													ROW
16	1	2	3	4	5	6							**16**
15	1	2	3	4	5	6							**15**
14	1	2	3	4	5	6							**14**
13	1	2	3	4	5	6							**13**
12	1	2	3	4	5	6	7						**12**
11	1	2	3	4	5	6	7	8					**11**
10	1	2	3	4	5	6	7	8	9	10			**10**
9	1	2	3	4	5	6	7	8	9	10	11		**9**
8	1	2	3	4	5	6	7	8	9	10	11		**8**
7	1	2	3	4	5	6	7	8	9	10	11		**7**
6	1	2	3	4	5	6	7	8	9	10	11	12	**6**
5	1	2	3	4	5	6	7	8	9	10	11	12	**5**
4	1	2	3	4	5	6	7	8	9	10	11	12	**4**
3	1	2	3	4	5	6	7	8	9	10	11	12	**3**
2	1	2	3	4	5	6	7	8	9	10	11	12	**2**
1	1	2	3	4	5	6	7	8	9	10	11	12	**1**

 = View of home plate or pitcher's mound is obstructed

home plate

Section 14

Infield Grandstand
Face Value of tickets is $45

Section 14 is down the first base
line behind Loge Boxes 106-110
and Field Boxes 20-23.

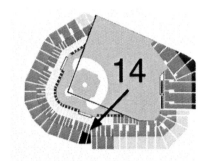

It is located behind first base
and the home dugout, and an
aisle runs down the middle of the section. Because of the aisle
you may have seats that are numbered consecutively but are
actually across the aisle from one another.

Pole issues in Section 14 are limited to the left side of the section
if you are facing the field. If you are seated anywhere to the right
of the aisle you will have a clear view.

The view from the center of Section 14

Section 14

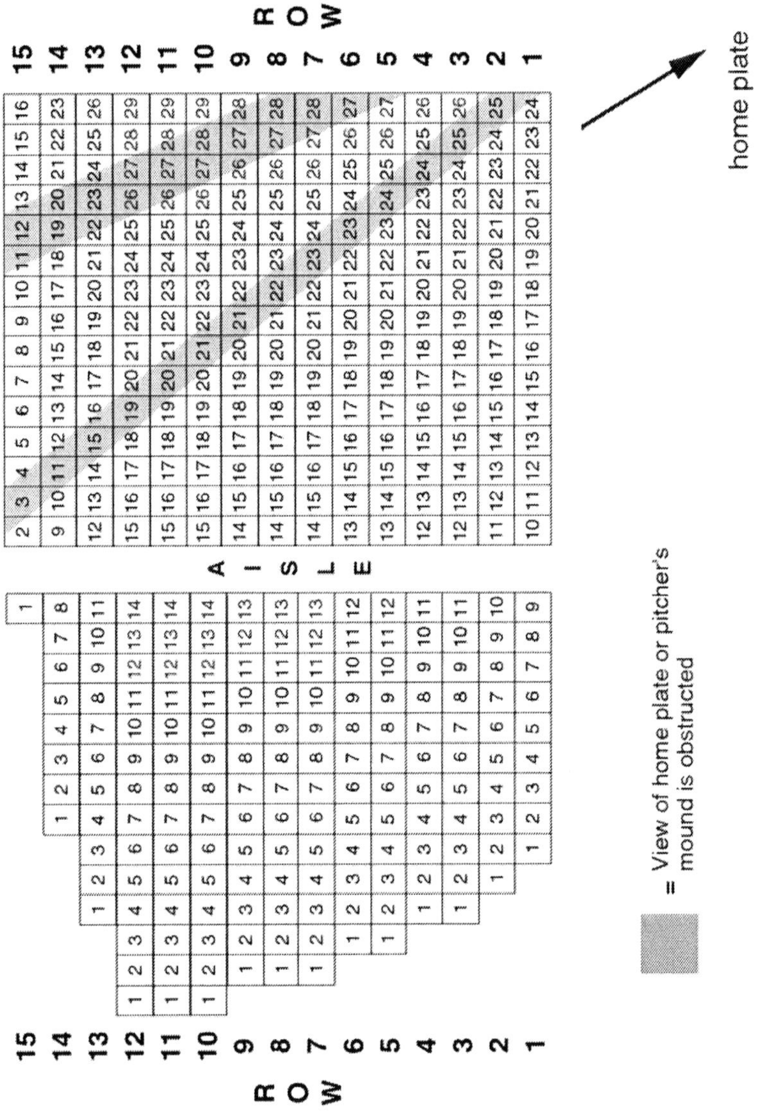

→ home plate

ROW

Seat-rating grid (ROW 15 at top → ROW 1 at bottom):

15	23	23	26	29	29	29	28	28	28	27	26	26	25	24
14	22	25	28	28	28	27	27	27	26	26	25	25	24	23
13	21	24	27	27	26	26	26	26	25	24	24	23	23	22
12	20	23	26	26	25	25	24	24	24	23	23	22	21	21
11	19	22	25	25	25	24	23	23	23	23	22	21	20	20
10	18	21	24	24	24	23	23	23	22	22	21	21	20	19
9	17	20	23	23	23	22	21	21	21	20	20	19	18	18
8	16	19	22	22	22	21	20	20	20	19	19	18	17	17
7	15	18	21	21	21	20	19	19	19	18	17	16	16	15
6	14	17	20	20	20	19	18	18	18	17	16	15	15	14
5	13	16	19	19	19	18	17	17	17	16	16	15	14	13
4	12	15	18	18	18	17	16	16	16	15	15	14	14	13
3	11	14	17	17	17	16	16	16	15	15	14	14	13	13
2	10	13	16	16	16	15	15	15	14	14	13	13	12	12
1	9	12	15	15	15	14	14	14	13	13	12	12	11	10

AISLE

Seat map (ROW 15 at top → ROW 1 at bottom):

ROW													
15	1												
14	8	7	6	5	4	3	2	1					
13	11	10	9	8	7	6	5	4	3	2	1		
12	14	13	12	11	10	9	8	7	6	5	4	3	2	1
11	14	13	12	11	10	9	8	7	6	5	4	3	2	1
10	14	13	12	11	10	9	8	7	6	5	4	3	2	1
9	13	12	11	10	9	8	7	6	5	4	3	2	1	
8	13	12	11	10	9	8	7	6	5	4	3	2	1	
7	13	12	11	10	9	8	7	6	5	4	3	2	1	
6	12	11	10	9	8	7	6	5	4	3	2	1		
5	12	11	10	9	8	7	6	5	4	3	2	1		
4	11	10	9	8	7	6	5	4	3	2	1			
3	11	10	9	8	7	6	5	4	3	2	1			
2	10	9	8	7	6	5	4	3	2	1				
1	9	8	7	6	5	4	3	2	1					

ROW

= View of home plate or pitcher's mound is obstructed

Section 15

Infield Grandstand
Face Value of tickets is $45

Section 15 is down the first base
line behind Loge Boxes 111-114
and Field Boxes 24-28.

It is located in between home
plate and first base and provides
an excellent view of the field and the entire park.

Pole issues are limited to the left side of the section if you are
facing the field.

The view from the center of Section 15

Section 15

ROW		Seats		ROW
19		1 2 3 4 5 6 7 8 9 10 11 12 13 14 15 16 17 18 19 20 21 22 23 24		19
18		1 2 3 4 5 6 7 8 9 10 11 12 13 14 15 16 17 18 19 20 21 22 23 24		18
17		1 2 3 4 5 6 7 8 9 10 11 12 13 14 15 16 17 18 19 20 21 22 23 24		17
16		1 2 3 4 5 6 7 8 9 10 11 12 13 14 15 16 17 18 19 20 21 22 23		16
15		1 2 3 4 5 6 7 8 9 10 11 12 13 14 15 16 17 18 19 20 21 22 23		15
14		1 2 3 4 5 6 7 8 9 10 11 12 13 14 15 16 17 18 19 20 21 22 23 24		14
13		1 2 3 4 5 6 7 8 9 10 11 12 13 14 15 16 17 18 19 20 21 22 23 24		13
12		1 2 3 4 5 6 7 8 9 10 11 12 13 14 15 16 17 18 19 20 21 22 23 24		12
R 11		1 2 3 4 5 6 7 8 9 10 11 12 13 14 15 16 17 18 19 20 21 22 23 24		11 R
O 10		1 2 3 4 5 6 7 8 9 10 11 12 13 14 15 16 17 18 19 20 21 22 23 24		10 O
W 9		1 2 3 4 5 6 7 8 9 10 11 12 13 14 15 16 17 18 19 20 21 22 23 24		9 W
8		1 2 3 4 5 6 7 8 9 10 11 12 13 14 15 16 17 18 19 20 21 22 23 24		8
7		1 2 3 4 5 6 7 8 9 10 11 12 13 14 15 16 17 18 19 20 21 22 23 24		7
6		1 2 3 4 5 6 7 8 9 10 11 12 13 14 15 16 17 18 19 20 21 22 23 24		6
5		1 2 3 4 5 6 7 8 9 10 11 12 13 14 15 16 17 18 19 20 21 22 23 24		5
4		1 2 3 4 5 6 7 8 9 10 11 12 13 14 15 16 17 18 19 20 21 22 23 24		4
3		1 2 3 4 5 6 7 8 9 10 11 12 13 14 15 16 17 18 19 20 21 22 23 24		3
2		1 2 3 4 5 6 7 8 9 10 11 12 13 14 15 16 17 18 19 20 21 22 23 24		2
1		1 2 3 4 5 6 7 8 9 10 11 12 13 14 15 16 17 18 19 20 21 22 23		1

 = View of home plate or pitcher's mound is obstructed

home plate

Section 16

Infield Grandstand
Face Value of tickets is $45

Section 16 is on the first base
line behind Loge Boxes 115-118
and Field Boxes 29-32.

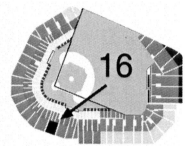

It is located in between home
plate and first base and provides an excellent view of the field
and the entire park.

Pole issues are limited to the left side of the section if you are
facing the field.

The view from the center of Section 16

Section 16

ROW																											ROW
19		1 2 3 4 5 6 7 8 9 10 11 12 13 14 15 16 17 18 19 20 21 22 23 24																									19
18		1 2 3 4 5 6 7 8 9 10 11 12 13 14 15 16 17 18 19 20 21 22 23 24																									18
17		1 2 3 4 5 6 7 8 9 10 11 12 13 14 15 16 17 18 19 20 21 22 23 24																									17
16	1 2 3 4 5 6 7 8 9 10 11 12 13 14 15 16 17 18 19 20 21 22 23 24 25 26																										16
15	1 2 3 4 5 6 7 8 9 10 11 12 13 14 15 16 17 18 19 20 21 22 23 24 25 26																										15
14	1 2 3 4 5 6 7 8 9 10 11 12 13 14 15 16 17 18 19 20 21 22 23 24 25 26																										14
13	1 2 3 4 5 6 7 8 9 10 11 12 13 14 15 16 17 18 19 20 21 22 23 24 25 26																										13
12	1 2 3 4 5 6 7 8 9 10 11 12 13 14 15 16 17 18 19 20 21 22 23 24 25 26																										12
11	1 2 3 4 5 6 7 8 9 10 11 12 13 14 15 16 17 18 19 20 21 22 23 24 25 26																										11
10	1 2 3 4 5 6 7 8 9 10 11 12 13 14 15 16 17 18 19 20 21 22 23 24 25 26																										10
9	1 2 3 4 5 6 7 8 9 10 11 12 13 14 15 16 17 18 19 20 21 22 23 24 25 26																										9
8	1 2 3 4 5 6 7 8 9 10 11 12 13 14 15 16 17 18 19 20 21 22 23 24 25 26																										8
7	1 2 3 4 5 6 7 8 9 10 11 12 13 14 15 16 17 18 19 20 21 22 23 24 25 26																										7
6	1 2 3 4 5 6 7 8 9 10 11 12 13 14 15 16 17 18 19 20 21 22 23 24 25 26																										6
5	1 2 3 4 5 6 7 8 9 10 11 12 13 14 15 16 17 18 19 20 21 22 23 24 25 26																										5
4	1 2 3 4 5 6 7 8 9 10 11 12 13 14 15 16 17 18 19 20 21 22 23 24 25 26																										4
3	1 2 3 4 5 6 7 8 9 10 11 12 13 14 15 16 17 18 19 20 21 22 23 24 25 26																										3
2	1 2 3 4 5 6 7 8 9 10 11 12 13 14 15 16 17 18 19 20 21 22 23 24 25 26																										2
1	1 2 3 4 5 6 7 8 9 10 11 12 13 14 15 16 17 18 19 20 21 22 23 24 25 26																										1

 = View of home plate or pitcher's mound is obstructed

home plate

Section 17

Infield Grandstand
Face Value of tickets is $45

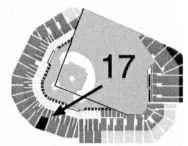

Section 17 is near the Sox on
deck circle behind Loge Boxes
119-122 and Field Boxes 33-36.

The view from the center of the
section is straight down the third base line. It is one of the better
sections to sit in, because there are very few seats with pole issues
and there are also no home plate screen issues.

Pole issues are limited to a few seats on the right side of the
section if you are facing the field.

The view from the center of Section 17

Section 17

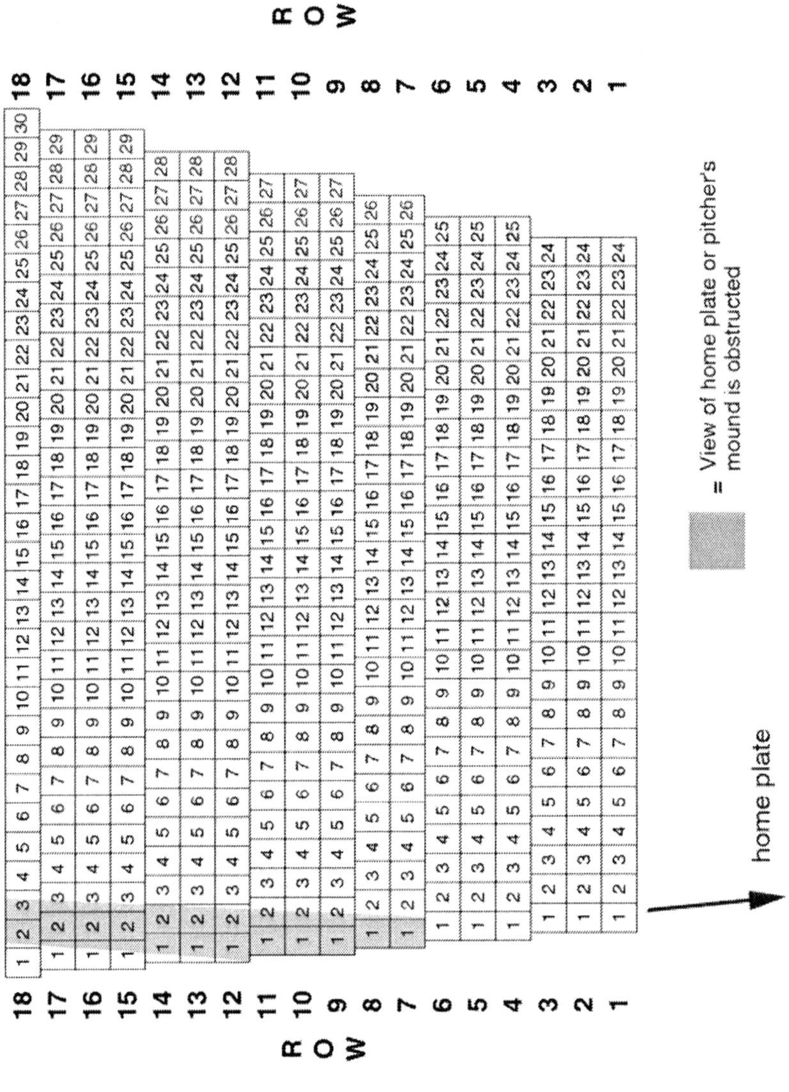

ROW

home plate

▓ = View of home plate or pitcher's mound is obstructed

Section 18

Infield Grandstand
Face Value of tickets is $45

Section 18 is near home plate
behind Loge Boxes 123-125 and
Field Boxes 38-40.

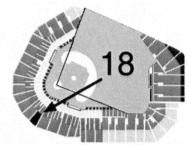

The vast majority of the seats in
this section are very good, as they can rightly be described as
being "behind home plate." Some of the seats on the left side of
the section facing the field have the home plate foul ball screen
to look through, which can be a minor annoyance.

There is a pole that obstructs the view of seats 4, 5, 6, or 7 in
most of the rows.

The view from the center of Section 18

Section 18

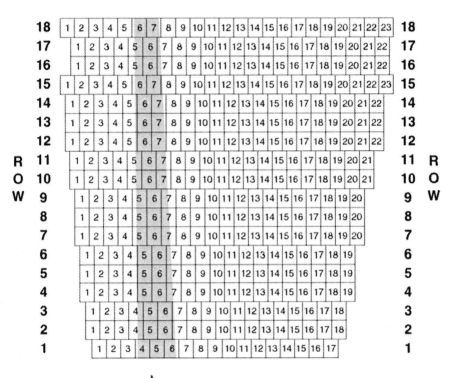

 = View of home plate or pitcher's mound is obstructed

home plate

Section 19

Infield Grandstand
Face Value of tickets is $45

Section 19 is near home plate
behind Loge Boxes 126-128 and
Field Boxes 40-41.

Section 19 is one of the best
sections in the entire park. Gloriously free from any pole
obstructions, it is behind home plate and offers a great view of
everything. The only minor annoyance could be looking through
the foul ball screen.

There are no pole issues in Section 19. Along with Section 21, it
is one of only two Grandstand Sections in the park completely
unaffected by poles.

The view from the center of Section 19

Section 19

ROW																									ROW
18	1	2	3	4	5	6	7	8	9	10	11	12	13	14	15	16	17	18	19	20	21	22	23		**18**
17	1	2	3	4	5	6	7	8	9	10	11	12	13	14	15	16	17	18	19	20	21	22	23		**17**
16	1	2	3	4	5	6	7	8	9	10	11	12	13	14	15	16	17	18	19	20	21	22	23		**16**
15	1	2	3	4	5	6	7	8	9	10	11	12	13	14	15	16	17	18	19	20	21	22			**15**
14	1	2	3	4	5	6	7	8	9	10	11	12	13	14	15	16	17	18	19	20	21	22			**14**
13		1	2	3	4	5	6	7	8	9	10	11	12	13	14	15	16	17	18	19	20	21			**13**
12		1	2	3	4	5	6	7	8	9	10	11	12	13	14	15	16	17	18	19	20	21			**12**
11		1	2	3	4	5	6	7	8	9	10	11	12	13	14	15	16	17	18	19	20				**11**
10		1	2	3	4	5	6	7	8	9	10	11	12	13	14	15	16	17	18	19	20				**10**
9			1	2	3	4	5	6	7	8	9	10	11	12	13	14	15	16	17	18	19				**9**
8			1	2	3	4	5	6	7	8	9	10	11	12	13	14	15	16	17	18	19				**8**
7			1	2	3	4	5	6	7	8	9	10	11	12	13	14	15	16	17	18	19				**7**
6				1	2	3	4	5	6	7	8	9	10	11	12	13	14	15	16	17	18				**6**
5				1	2	3	4	5	6	7	8	9	10	11	12	13	14	15	16	17	18				**5**
4				1	2	3	4	5	6	7	8	9	10	11	12	13	14	15	16	17	18				**4**
3					1	2	3	4	5	6	7	8	9	10	11	12	13	14	15	16	17				**3**
2					1	2	3	4	5	6	7	8	9	10	11	12	13	14	15	16	17				**2**
1					1	2	3	4	5	6	7	8	9	10	11	12	13	14	15	16	17				**1**

There are no pole obstructions in Section 19

home plate

Section 20

Infield Grandstand
Face Value of tickets is $45

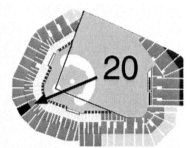

Section 20 is in back of home plate behind Loge Boxes 129-130 and Field Boxes 42-44.

Section 20 is one of the best sections in the entire park. It is behind home plate and offers a great view of everything. The only minor annoyance could be looking through the foul ball screen.

Pole issues in Section 20 are limited to seats 1 and 2 in rows 3 through 18. Any seat numbered 4 or higher is safe from poles.

The view from the center of Section 20

Section 20

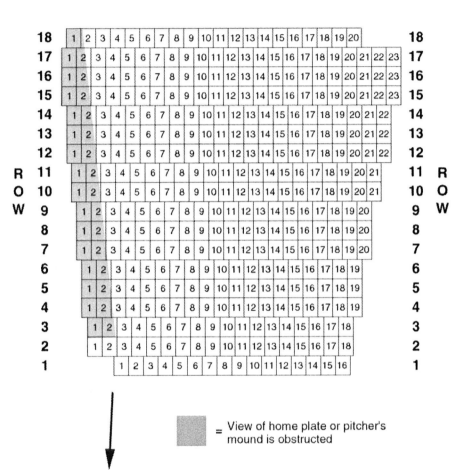

= View of home plate or pitcher's mound is obstructed

home plate

Section 21

Infield Grandstand
Face Value of tickets is $45

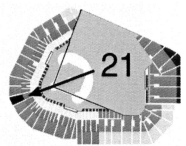

Section 21 is near home plate
behind Loge Boxes 130-131 and
Field Boxes 45-47.

Section 21 is one of the best
sections in the entire park. Gloriously free from any pole
obstructions, it is behind home plate and offers a great view of
everything. The only minor annoyance could be looking through
the foul ball screen.

There are no pole issues in Section 21. Along with Section 19, it
is one of only two Grandstand Sections in the park completely
unaffected by poles.

The view from the center of Section 21

Section 21

ROW																									ROW
16	1	2	3	4	5	6	7	8	9	10	11	12	13	14	15	16	17	18	19	20	21	22	23		**16**
15	1	2	3	4	5	6	7	8	9	10	11	12	13	14	15	16	17	18	19	20	21	22	23		**15**
14	1	2	3	4	5	6	7	8	9	10	11	12	13	14	15	16	17	18	19	20	21	22		**14**
13	1	2	3	4	5	6	7	8	9	10	11	12	13	14	15	16	17	18	19	20	21	22		**13**
12	1	2	3	4	5	6	7	8	9	10	11	12	13	14	15	16	17	18	19	20	21		**12**
11	1	2	3	4	5	6	7	8	9	10	11	12	13	14	15	16	17	18	19	20	21		**11**
10	1	2	3	4	5	6	7	8	9	10	11	12	13	14	15	16	17	18	19	20	21		**10**
9	1	2	3	4	5	6	7	8	9	10	11	12	13	14	15	16	17	18	19	20		**9**
8	1	2	3	4	5	6	7	8	9	10	11	12	13	14	15	16	17	18	19	20		**8**
7	1	2	3	4	5	6	7	8	9	10	11	12	13	14	15	16	17	18	19	20		**7**
6	1	2	3	4	5	6	7	8	9	10	11	12	13	14	15	16	17	18	19		**6**
5	1	2	3	4	5	6	7	8	9	10	11	12	13	14	15	16	17	18	19		**5**
4	1	2	3	4	5	6	7	8	9	10	11	12	13	14	15	16	17	18		**4**
3	1	2	3	4	5	6	7	8	9	10	11	12	13	14	15	16	17	18		**3**
2	1	2	3	4	5	6	7	8	9	10	11	12	13	14	15	16	17	18		**2**
1	1	2	3	4	5	6	7	8	9	10	11	12	13	14	15	16	17		**1**

There are no pole obstructions in Section 21

home plate

Section 22

Infield Grandstand
Face Value of tickets is $45

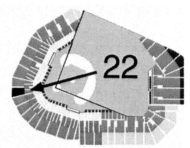

Section 22 is in back of home
plate behind Loge Boxes 132-
134 and Field Boxes 48-49.

Section 22 is one of the better
sections in the entire park. It is behind home plate on the third
base side and offers a great view of everything. The only minor
annoyance could be looking through the foul ball screen.

Pole issues in Section 22 are limited to seats 1 and, in come
cases, 2 in rows 2 through 16. Any seat numbered 3 or higher is
safe from poles.

The view from the center of Section 22

Section 22

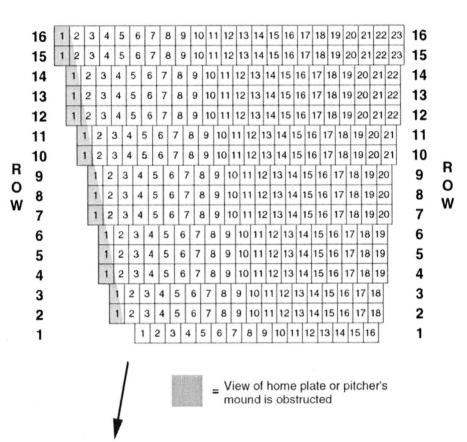

= View of home plate or pitcher's mound is obstructed

home plate

Section 23

Infield Grandstand
Face Value of tickets is $45

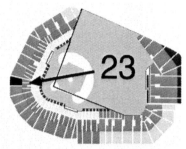

Section 23 is near home plate
and behind Loge Boxes 135-136
and Field Boxes 50-51.

Section 23 is an excellent
section. It is near home plate and offers a great view of the entire
park.

There is a pole which obstructs the view the higher numbered
seats on the end of the rows. Any seat numbered 15 or lower is
safe from poles.

The view from the center of Section 23

Section 23

ROW		Seats		ROW
17		1 2 3 4 5 6 7 8 9 10 11 12 13 14 15 16 17 18 19 20 21 22 23		**17**
16		1 2 3 4 5 6 7 8 9 10 11 12 13 14 15 16 17 18 19 20 21 22		**16**
15		1 2 3 4 5 6 7 8 9 10 11 12 13 14 15 16 17 18 19 20 21 22 23		**15**
14		1 2 3 4 5 6 7 8 9 10 11 12 13 14 15 16 17 18 19 20 21 22		**14**
13		1 2 3 4 5 6 7 8 9 10 11 12 13 14 15 16 17 18 19 20 21 22		**13**
12		1 2 3 4 5 6 7 8 9 10 11 12 13 14 15 16 17 18 19 20 21		**12**
11		1 2 3 4 5 6 7 8 9 10 11 12 13 14 15 16 17 18 19 20 21		**11**
10		1 2 3 4 5 6 7 8 9 10 11 12 13 14 15 16 17 18 19 20 21		**10**
9		1 2 3 4 5 6 7 8 9 10 11 12 13 14 15 16 17 18 19 20		**9**
8		1 2 3 4 5 6 7 8 9 10 11 12 13 14 15 16 17 18 19 20		**8**
7		1 2 3 4 5 6 7 8 9 10 11 12 13 14 15 16 17 18 19 20		**7**
6		1 2 3 4 5 6 7 8 9 10 11 12 13 14 15 16 17 18 19		**6**
5		1 2 3 4 5 6 7 8 9 10 11 12 13 14 15 16 17 18 19		**5**
4		1 2 3 4 5 6 7 8 9 10 11 12 13 14 15 16 17 18		**4**
3		1 2 3 4 5 6 7 8 9 10 11 12 13 14 15 16 17 18		**3**
2		1 2 3 4 5 6 7 8 9 10 11 12 13 14 15 16 17 18		**2**
1		1 2 3 4 5 6 7 8 9 10 11 12 13 14 15 16		**1**

R O W (left) / **R O W** (right)

= View of home plate or pitcher's mound is obstructed

home plate

Section 24

Infield Grandstand
Face Value of tickets is $45

Section 24 is near the visiting
team's on deck circle and behind
Loge Boxes 137-140 and Field
Boxes 51-55.

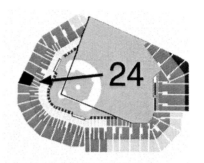

Section 24 is one of the best Grandstand sections in the park for
viewing a game. Seats in the center of the section look directly
down the first base line and are very close to the action.

Only a handful of seats in the upper rows at the very end of each
row are affected by pole issues.

The view from the center of Section 24

Section 24

ROW

18 17 16 15 14 13 12 11 10 9 8 7 6 5 4 3 2 1

(seating chart grid for Section 24, with row numbers 1–18 and seat numbers increasing toward the upper rows; shaded seats marked with # indicate obstructed views)

home plate

= View of home plate or pitcher's mound is obstructed

Section 25

Infield Grandstand
Face Value of tickets is $45

Section 25 is in between home
plate and third base and behind
Loge Boxes 141-144 and Field
Boxes 56-60.

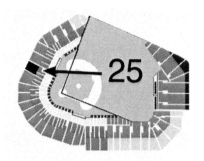

Section 25 is an excellent section for viewing the game. With the
vast majority of the seats free from obstructions, you really have a
nice view of the infield and the entire park from this section.

Only the first two seats in each row have pole issues.

The view from the center of Section 25

Section 25

ROW	1	2	3	4	5	6	7	8	9	10	11	12	13	14	15	16	17	18	19	20	21	22	23	24	ROW
16	1	2	3	4	5	6	7	8	9	10	11	12	13	14	15	16	17	18	19	20	21	22	23		16
15	1	2	3	4	5	6	7	8	9	10	11	12	13	14	15	16	17	18	19	20	21	22	23	24	15
14	1	2	3	4	5	6	7	8	9	10	11	12	13	14	15	16	17	18	19	20	21	22	23	24	14
13	1	2	3	4	5	6	7	8	9	10	11	12	13	14	15	16	17	18	19	20	21	22	23	24	13
12	1	2	3	4	5	6	7	8	9	10	11	12	13	14	15	16	17	18	19	20	21	22	23	24	12
11	1	2	3	4	5	6	7	8	9	10	11	12	13	14	15	16	17	18	19	20	21	22	23	24	11
10	1	2	3	4	5	6	7	8	9	10	11	12	13	14	15	16	17	18	19	20	21	22	23	24	10
9	1	2	3	4	5	6	7	8	9	10	11	12	13	14	15	16	17	18	19	20	21	22	23	24	9
8	1	2	3	4	5	6	7	8	9	10	11	12	13	14	15	16	17	18	19	20	21	22	23	24	8
7	1	2	3	4	5	6	7	8	9	10	11	12	13	14	15	16	17	18	19	20	21	22	23	24	7
6	1	2	3	4	5	6	7	8	9	10	11	12	13	14	15	16	17	18	19	20	21	22	23	24	6
5	1	2	3	4	5	6	7	8	9	10	11	12	13	14	15	16	17	18	19	20	21	22	23	24	5
4	1	2	3	4	5	6	7	8	9	10	11	12	13	14	15	16	17	18	19	20	21	22	23	24	4
3	1	2	3	4	5	6	7	8	9	10	11	12	13	14	15	16	17	18	19	20	21	22	23	24	3
2	1	2	3	4	5	6	7	8	9	10	11	12	13	14	15	16	17	18	19	20	21	22	23	24	2
1		1	2	3	4	5	6	7	8	9	10	11	12	13	14	15	16	17	18	19	20	21	22	23	1

home plate

 = View of home plate or pitcher's mound is obstructed

Section 26

Infield Grandstand
Face Value of tickets is $45

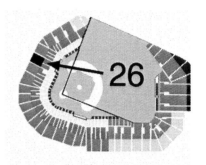

Section 26 is near third base and
the visiting team's dugout. It is
behind Loge Boxes 145-148 and
Field Boxes 61-64.

Section 26 is a very good section for viewing the game. It is very
close to the infield but also has a nice view of the Monster.

Pole issues in this section run diagonally from bottom right to
seats in the middle of the top rows if you are facing the field. The
pole issues in the first few rows with the lowest seat numbers are
particularly problematic. The first two seats in rows 10 through
18 are also obstructed.

The view from the center of Section 26

Section 26

ROW																									ROW
18	1	2	3	4	5	6	7	8	9	10	11	12	13	14	15	16	17	18	19	20	21	22	23	24	18
17	1	2	3	4	5	6	7	8	9	10	11	12	13	14	15	16	17	18	19	20	21	22	23	24	17
16	1	2	3	4	5	6	7	8	9	10	11	12	13	14	15	16	17	18	19	20	21	22	23		16
15	1	2	3	4	5	6	7	8	9	10	11	12	13	14	15	16	17	18	19	20	21	22	23	24	15
14	1	2	3	4	5	6	7	8	9	10	11	12	13	14	15	16	17	18	19	20	21	22	23	24	14
13	1	2	3	4	5	6	7	8	9	10	11	12	13	14	15	16	17	18	19	20	21	22	23	24	13
12	1	2	3	4	5	6	7	8	9	10	11	12	13	14	15	16	17	18	19	20	21	22	23	24	12
11	1	2	3	4	5	6	7	8	9	10	11	12	13	14	15	16	17	18	19	20	21	22	23	24	11
10	1	2	3	4	5	6	7	8	9	10	11	12	13	14	15	16	17	18	19	20	21	22	23	24	10
9	1	2	3	4	5	6	7	8	9	10	11	12	13	14	15	16	17	18	19	20	21	22	23	24	9
8	1	2	3	4	5	6	7	8	9	10	11	12	13	14	15	16	17	18	19	20	21	22	23	24	8
7	1	2	3	4	5	6	7	8	9	10	11	12	13	14	15	16	17	18	19	20	21	22	23	24	7
6	1	2	3	4	5	6	7	8	9	10	11	12	13	14	15	16	17	18	19	20	21	22	23	24	6
5	1	2	3	4	5	6	7	8	9	10	11	12	13	14	15	16	17	18	19	20	21	22	23	24	5
4	1	2	3	4	5	6	7	8	9	10	11	12	13	14	15	16	17	18	19	20	21	22	23	24	4
3	1	2	3	4	5	6	7	8	9	10	11	12	13	14	15	16	17	18	19	20	21	22	23	24	3
2	1	2	3	4	5	6	7	8	9	10	11	12	13	14	15	16	17	18	19	20	21	22	23	24	2
1		1	2	3	4	5	6	7	8	9	10	11	12	13	14	15	16	17	18	19	20	21	22	23	1

home plate

▨ = View of home plate or pitcher's mound is obstructed

Section 27

Infield Grandstand
Face Value of tickets is $45

Section 27 is just past third base
on the left field line. It is behind
Loge Boxes 149-151 and Field
Boxes 65-68.

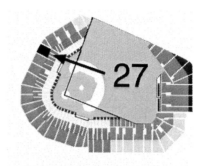

Section 27 is a very good section
for viewing the game. It is close to the infield but also has a good
view of the Monster.

Pole issues in this section run diagonally from bottom right to
top left if you are facing the field. The pole issues in the first few
rows with the lowest seat numbers are particularly problematic.

The view from the center of Section 27

Section 27

ROW		Seats																								ROW
18	1	2	3	4	5	6	7	8	9	10	11	12	13	14	15	16	17	18	19	20	21	22	23	24		**18**
17	1	2	3	4	5	6	7	8	9	10	11	12	13	14	15	16	17	18	19	20	21	22	23	24		**17**
16	1	2	3	4	5	6	7	8	9	10	11	12	13	14	15	16	17	18	19	20	21	22	23	24		**16**
15	1	2	3	4	5	6	7	8	9	10	11	12	13	14	15	16	17	18	19	20	21	22	23	24		**15**
14	1	2	3	4	5	6	7	8	9	10	11	12	13	14	15	16	17	18	19	20	21	22	23	24		**14**
13	1	2	3	4	5	6	7	8	9	10	11	12	13	14	15	16	17	18	19	20	21	22	23	24	25	**13**
12	1	2	3	4	5	6	7	8	9	10	11	12	13	14	15	16	17	18	19	20	21	22	23	24	25	**12**
11	1	2	3	4	5	6	7	8	9	10	11	12	13	14	15	16	17	18	19	20	21	22	23	24	25	**11**
10	1	2	3	4	5	6	7	8	9	10	11	12	13	14	15	16	17	18	19	20	21	22	23	24	25	**10**
9	1	2	3	4	5	6	7	8	9	10	11	12	13	14	15	16	17	18	19	20	21	22	23	24	25	**9**
8	1	2	3	4	5	6	7	8	9	10	11	12	13	14	15	16	17	18	19	20	21	22	23	24	25	**8**
7	1	2	3	4	5	6	7	8	9	10	11	12	13	14	15	16	17	18	19	20	21	22	23	24	25	**7**
6	1	2	3	4	5	6	7	8	9	10	11	12	13	14	15	16	17	18	19	20	21	22	23	24	25	**6**
5	1	2	3	4	5	6	7	8	9	10	11	12	13	14	15	16	17	18	19	20	21	22	23	24	25	**5**
4	1	2	3	4	5	6	7	8	9	10	11	12	13	14	15	16	17	18	19	20	21	22	23	24	25	**4**
3	1	2	3	4	5	6	7	8	9	10	11	12	13	14	15	16	17	18	19	20	21	22	23	24	25	**3**
2	1	2	3	4	5	6	7	8	9	10	11	12	13	14	15	16	17	18	19	20	21	22	23	24	25	**2**
1		1	2	3	4	5	6	7	8	9	10	11	12	13	14	15	16	17	18	19	20	21	22	23		**1**

 = View of home plate or pitcher's mound is obstructed

home plate

Section 28

Infield Grandstand
Face Value of tickets is $45

Section 28 is in just past third
base on the left field line and is
behind Loge Box 152 and Field
Box 69.

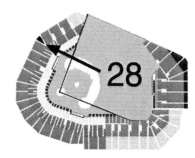

Perhaps the most oddly shaped
section in the park, 28 is basically a triangle. The first row is Row
3 and it has only one seat. The unusual shape is due to the fact
that 28 is the junction between the sections that are parallel to
the third base line (24-27) and the sections that turn so they can
face the infield (29-33).

Pole issues are limited to upper row seats on the left and right
sides of the section.

The view from the center of Section 28

Section 28

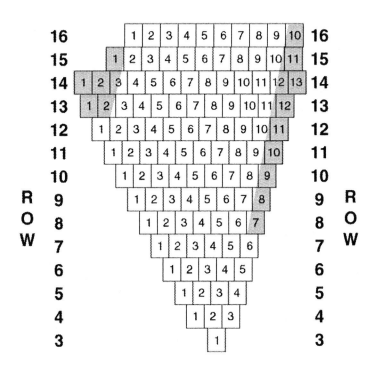

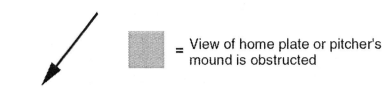

= View of home plate or pitcher's mound is obstructed

home plate

Section 29

Infield Grandstand
Face Value of tickets is $45

Section 29 is past third base on
the left field line and is behind
Loge Boxes 153-156 and Field
Boxes 70-71.

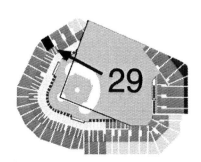

It is an excellent section for
viewing the game. The seats are close to the Green Monster and
you are still fairly close to the infield.

A pole affects seats 1 and 2 in the first row and the obstruction
runs diagonally up to seats 5 and 6 in row 18. The last seat in
rows 3 and 4 are also affected.

The view from the center of Section 29

Section 29

home plate

= View of home plate or pitcher's mound is obstructed

Section 30

Infield Grandstand
Face Value of tickets is $45

Section 30 is on the left field line
between third base and the Green
Monster and is behind Loge
Boxes 157-159 and Field Boxes
72-76.

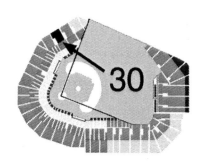

It is a very good section for viewing the game. The seats are close
to the Green Monster and not too far from the infield.

Only a few seats have pole issues. If you are facing the field these
are on the right side of the section in rows 8 through 15. Seat 19
in row 2 is also affected.

The view from the center of Section 30

Section 30

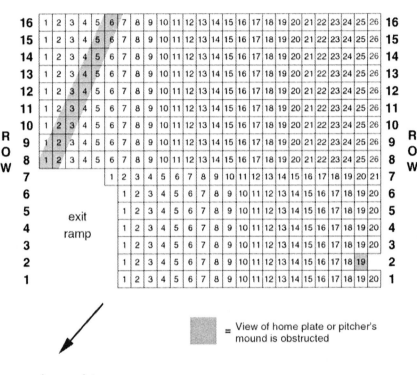

= View of home plate or pitcher's mound is obstructed

home plate

Section 31

Infield Grandstand
Face Value of tickets is $45

Section 31 is on the left field line
near the Green Monster and is
behind Loge Boxes 160-161 and
Field Boxes 77-82.

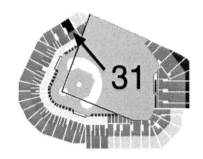

While it is a good section for viewing the game, be aware that it
is further from home plate than any other section on the left side
that is classified as Infield Grandstand. If you are one section
over in Section 32, the face value of tickets drops to $27.

If you are facing the field, pole issues are limited to seats on the
right in rows 8 through 16. All seats in the first 7 rows are not
affected by poles, and in rows 8 through 16, any seats numbered
higher than 11 are safe from poles.

The view from the center of Section 31

Section 31

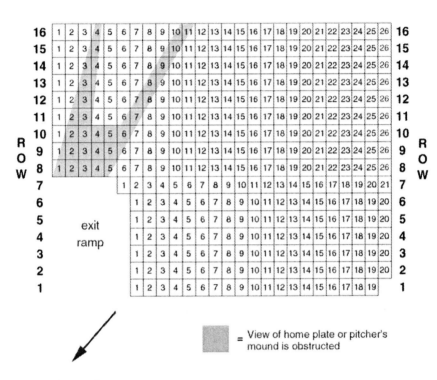

home plate

= View of home plate or pitcher's mound is obstructed

Section 32

Outfield Grandstand
Face Value of tickets is $27
No alcohol section

Section 32 is on the left field line
near the Green Monster and is
behind Loge Box 162-163.

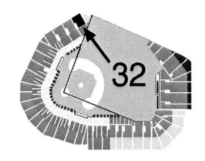

Along with section 33, this is one of best value sections in the
park. With seats priced at only $27, it is in an excellent position
to view the game and the entire park. There are Loge Box seats in
front of Section 32, but no Field Box seats, which makes these
seats some of the closest to the field of any grandstand section.

Rows 1 through 7 are not affected by poles, but some seats on
the right side of the section if you are facing the field are
affected. Please be aware that seats 3 through 6 in row 1 are often
affected by wheelchair seating in front of them.

The view from the center of Section 32

Section 32

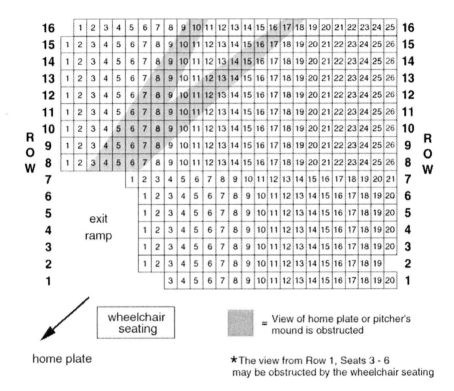

	16		1	2	3	4	5	6	7	8	9	10	11	12	13	14	15	16	17	18	19	20	21	22	23	24	25		16

wheelchair seating

= View of home plate or pitcher's mound is obstructed

home plate

★The view from Row 1, Seats 3 - 6 may be obstructed by the wheelchair seating

Section 33

Outfield Grandstand
Face Value of tickets is $27
No alcohol section

Section 33 is down the left field
line next to the Green Monster
and behind Loge Box 163.

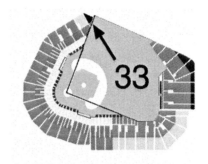

33 is a triangular treasure tucked into the left field corner next to
the Monster. It is the only Grandstand section not covered by a
roof. It is the closest Grandstand section to the field, with only 1
to 3 rows of Loge Box seats in front of it. And, if you sit in row 3,
seat 16, you can actually touch the Monster and the left field foul
pole from your seat. This is the same pole off which Pudge Fisk
hit his classic 1975 World Series home run.

Pole issues in this section run across the middle rows. If you have
any seats in the first three rows you have no pole issues.

The view from the center of Section 33

Section 33

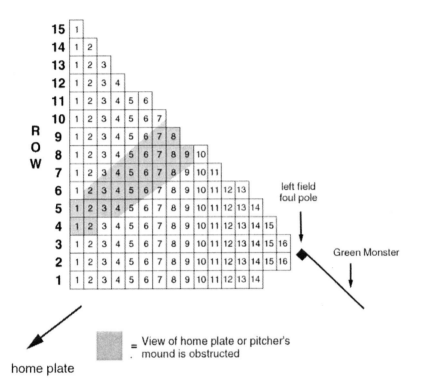

home plate

left field
foul pole

Green Monster

= View of home plate or pitcher's
  mound is obstructed

Notes

_____

_____

_____

_____

_____

_____

_____

_____

_____

Notes

Notes